A PLATFORM FOR THE
AMERICAN WAY

A Platform for the
AMERICAN WAY

by

HARLEY L. LUTZ, Ph.D., LL.D.,
PROFESSOR EMERITUS OF PUBLIC FINANCE
PRINCETON UNIVERSITY

APPLETON-CENTURY-CROFTS, INC.
NEW YORK

*To my grandchildren
and to all other children
of generations to come
who deserve to receive from
us the freedom we have inherited*

PREFACE

THIS IS AN unconventional sort of book. Instead of a few long chapters, it is a series of thumbnail sketches. It uses the short essay form, with a capsulized statement of each topic accompanied by a longer discussion.

But it is dogmatic, and intentionally so. There are too many wishy-washy compromisers today, too many who are not willing to take a positive stand. The editorial-like pieces in this book will provide fighting material for those who like a fight, whichever side they may be on.

The belief and philosophy expressed here are individualistic rather than socialistic. They are a defense of man against the state. It is high time that such a defense be prepared, for the issue of personal freedom transcends all other issues involving the future of mankind. Many fear where they are going but they think they lack control over their destiny; and they will have none unless a course is charted for them.

In the author's view we are both drifting, and being steered, into some form of the national socialist state. The drift results from citizen apathy, indifference, and ignorance of solutions. Solutions are offered here, and if no result other than active thought and discussion is provoked by the definitive principles stated in this book, a useful purpose will have been served.

But there is also steering, and crafty steering, toward the national socialist state by those who know exactly what they want and how to get it. Let none be deceived by the fair words and false promises of these pilots. If they succeed, there will be the terrors of confiscation and concentration camps. There are no racial or national differences in men drunk with power.

The pattern of national socialism and communism is already clear. It includes slavery for the masses, expropriation and liquidation for the middle and upper classes, and extraordinary privileges for those party members who have demonstrated outstanding inhuman qualities.

Time is running out, but national socialism can yet be defeated here if we begin to act and if we act together. This book offers a program for all who believe in freedom and who want to remain free here in America.

HARLEY L. LUTZ

Princeton, New Jersey. April, 1952

CONTENTS

PAGE

PREFACE vii

PART I. THE BASES OF FREEDOM 1

Freedom and Peace 1
The *Right* to Own 2
Stability and Permanence of the Social Order . . 4
Sound Financial Management 5
Public Debt Policy 7
The Public Debt Is Deferred Taxation 9
Tax Policy 11
Spending Policy 13
Efficiency and Economy 14

PART II. THE STATE, THE PARTY, AND THE PEOPLE . . 17

The Political Party System 17
Constitutional Checks and Balances 19
Functions of a Political Party 20
Platform or Candidate 22
The Independent Voter 23
Principle versus Expediency 25
Platform Integrity 26
More Government, or Less? 28
Freedom Through Less Government 30

PART III. THE PLATFORM 33

Section 1. The Road to Less Government 33

"Bring Government Back Home" 34
Federal Lending 35
Grants-in-aid 37
Subsidies 39
Subsidies for National Defense 41
Agricultural Subsidies 42
Direct Government Participation in Business . . 47
Reinterpret the General Welfare 51

ix

PAGE

Reduce Federal Personnel 53
Reorganize Departments and Agencies 54

Section 2. The Road to Better Government . . . 57

Better Government Through Less Government . . 57
The States Must Be Preserved 59
The Essentials of Government 61
National Defense and Security 62
A Free Economy Is the Strongest Economy . . 64
Paying as We Go 66
Foreign Policy 67

Section 3. The Road to Proper Federal Functions . . 70

Tests of Proper Federal Functions 71
Policing Economic and Business Activities . . . 72
Competition and Monopoly 75
Fair Price and Trade Practices 77
Informational Services 79
The Conservation of Natural Resources . . . 81
Public Education 83
Public Health 85
The Dependency Problem 89
Old Age and Survivors' Benefits 91
Public Assistance 95
Unemployment Compensation 98
The Federal Government as Trustee 100
Full Employment 103
Plant Seizure 107

CONCLUSION 111

A PLATFORM FOR THE
AMERICAN WAY

Part I

THE BASES OF FREEDOM

FREEDOM AND PEACE

The strength of America is the hope of the world for peace, freedom, and happiness. America's strength is both material and spiritual, in nature and origin. It comes from within, not without, and if it be sapped away, this will be by enemies within, rather than without, our gates.

In a world suffering from fear, enslavement, and despair, America stands like a bright beacon in the night. Her strength is a unique compound of economic materialism and spiritual idealism. The faith of her people includes a belief in the value and virtue of machinery, technology, and the significance of material possessions. It includes also such basic, but essentially ethical concepts as the worth and dignity of the individual, his right to life, liberty, and the pursuit of happiness, and the fundamental privilege of free men to select those by whom they shall be governed.

These materialistic and ethical concepts are older, by far, than our Constitution. They are older, even, than the record of settlement on this continent. They have been part of the stock in trade of political and moral philosophers for thousands of years. But they were never assembled together into a practical working pattern for men to live by until it was done here in America. The establishment of this pattern and the adherence to it through trials and tribulations are truly an expression of the genius of America.

It is right and proper that we should have both materialistic and spiritual aspirations. Though it has been said that man does not live by bread alone, this is a recognition that he must

1

have bread. The *right* to own property and to make contracts is the foundation of all other freedoms, yet this right itself is dependent upon preservation of the broad concept of freedom, for a mark of the unfree through the ages has been the incapacity, legally, to own property or to make contracts.

We have made these resources of material well-being and freedom our own through our energy and our will to be free. No alien force or power can take them from us. But we can lose them through our own neglect, sloth, and indifference. The siren songs of those who would make the state the master, the owner, the provider of all good things, have lured some and will draw others, if we let ourselves and our children forget the real sources of our strength and our freedom.

THE *Right* TO OWN

The keystone of the arch that supports America's material and spiritual strength is the *right* to own property. This *right* is the real badge of freedom. An untrammeled right of ownership must include freedom to buy, sell, or otherwise dispose of things owned. Hence freedom includes contract, which is the acceptance of obligations and commitments that are, in whatever form written, an expression of the right to deliver things of value to another, and to claim things of value from that other person.

THE PRIMARY contrast between free America and the nations that are enslaved behind the "iron curtain" is in the difference that exists with respect to the rights of property ownership. Here, any person is entirely free to own any kind of property— land, houses, insurance policies, savings deposits, the wages of his labor, and even a part of a large business corporation through acquisition of one or more shares of its stock. There, the state is the owner of all productive resources—land, factories, machinery, railroads, and so on, and the individual is severely limited as to the amount and kinds of possessions that he may call his own. He is not secure even in this limited possession. He can be sent to forced labor without wages, and even his holdings of furniture, clothing, state bonds, and currency are nominal ownership only, for these are subject to confiscation at the whim of the state.

The above proposition does not mean that all persons *do* own property, although, since wages and other income are property, there are few who have no direct experience with ownership. Nor does its validity require that all persons *must* be owners, although, again, there are few who do not enjoy unfettered possession of something, however small its value may be. The proposition does mean that all persons *can* own something, that they are free to become owners, and that in this fact lies the source and essence of all other freedoms.

The experience and record of history demonstrate the truth that property rights are the basis of all other rights. The first step toward enslavement of a conquered nation is the confiscation of property. This has happened with respect to a large proportion of all private property in all of the Soviet satellite states. On the other hand, enslavement has not always involved restrictions on religion and religious beliefs, although such restrictions have at times suited the Communist purpose. In other times and places slaves were permitted and encouraged to engage in religious rites and ceremonies. They could even marry but could never be sure of custody of offspring. They were never permitted, as slaves, to own property, for such ownership would involve obligations and commitments that unfree men could not lawfully make. The people behind the "iron curtain" vote, but that does not make them free. The first and most essential test of freedom in all its forms—political, spiritual, and economic—is the *right* to own property.

STABILITY AND PERMANENCE OF THE SOCIAL ORDER

As the main bulwark of a free society, the right of ownership requires stability and duration. There must be both assurance of security in possession and protection against confiscation at whim. There must be adequate faith that the social order can be preserved and that it will endure. Otherwise, ownership will have little value and with its passing as a prized right all other freedoms will crumble.

THE PRICE OF ownership, and hence the price of all freedoms to which the right of ownership is the key, is effort. We must work to become owners. But effort, being irksome, would slacken and not often lead to ownership, if there were no protection by a stable and enduring government. Brigandage, looting, spoliation public and private, would enrich a few while impoverishing the many. When the Roman authority collapsed and the barbarian hordes swept in, no property titles were secure or respected.

But government, by providing and assuring protection against confiscation, theft, and all other forms of disturbance and disorder, does not make men free. Government is not the source or origin of freedom, even though its power is the ultimate safeguard of ownership titles. Rather, government—in the true sense and not as dictatorship—is the means and the agency through which free men unite to express and exercise their freedom.

Much has been said and written about the alleged conflict between property rights and human rights. There is no conflict. Property, as such, has no rights, and the most important human right is the right to own property. Misunderstanding often arises from the failure to distinguish between the right or freedom to own and the obligations or restrictions on ownership essential to the protection of others in their exercise of this right. No concept of freedom would be valid which ignored the balancing and maintaining of the same and equal rights of all. For this we look to government, acting as the servant, not the master, of free men, to assure to all the equal protection of the law. This is an assertion, not a denial, of freedom.

Government's authority, and hence the degree to which it can provide protection for all, involves duration or permanence. We must assume its perpetuity. A terminal date would be the prelude to chaos. The advocates of overthrow or radical change plead for gradual, evolutionary development into what they promise will be a better world. The crucial test of all such doctrines and promises is the attitude on the right of ownership. In proportion as they would curtail the freedom of the right of ownership, they are limiting all freedom.

SOUND FINANCIAL MANAGEMENT

The most important condition for the stability and permanence of our own form of government here in the United States is the sound management of the public finances. If this condition is met consistently and properly, our prized freedoms will be secure. If it is not, these freedoms will be in grave danger, first, because the people will then be more responsive to the lying promises of the fifth columnists here, and second, because the nation will be more vulnerable to attack by a foreign enemy.

THE RECORDS of history supply abundant examples of the connection between sound financial policy and the stability and permanence of governments. Many small states have lost all, or virtually all, power of independent action as a result of excessive, unwise foreign loans. The German government that committed the inflationary excesses of the early 1920's did not survive the storm. The story of disastrous inflation in many places and over a long period is too well known to be repeated here.

Yet, notwithstanding the abundance of the record, it is necessary to be always on guard. Few fallacies have been more persistent, despite innumerable plain refutations, than the cheap money fallacy. This country's history provides many examples—the colonial land banks, Continental currency, wildcat banking, Greenbackism, Free Silver, gold devaluation, and "pegged" interest rates. Each of these was a case of trying to escape the plain facts and consequences of life, of trying to get something for nothing. In each instance it was an attempt to escape from debts, or taxes, or some other costs, that had been incurred without being fully weighed. The easy but futile way of lightening the burden was to cheapen the currency.

What is not perceived, in these crazes, is that while inflation may benefit some, it robs others. It is not a universal panacea. If debtors gain, creditors lose; if sellers gain, buyers lose; if speculators gain, those with fixed incomes lose. When a government is willing, or is forced by circumstance, to play some groups against other groups by resort to currency manipulation, it no longer commands the respect of any and it is likely to lose the support of all.

The real issue and the fundamental problem is to avoid debasement of the currency which is the universal standard of value. The first requisite is to avoid budget deficits, for any substantial rise of the public debt is, or will eventually lead to, a debasement of the currency. The obvious corollary is to levy taxes sufficient to cover all governmental spending. And here is the rub. It is so easy, by demagogic methods, to persuade the people that they can enjoy benefits now and pay later, merely by authorizing government to "put it on the cuff" instead of "on the line." What is this but another version of the age-old nonsense of getting something for nothing through fiscal trickery?

In these days when the United States stands virtually alone as the exponent and symbol of freedom, it is more important than ever that we demonstrate our capacity to face grave issues without resort to printing-press money.

PUBLIC DEBT POLICY

The primary test of the government's ability to manage its finances is in its debt policy. When a government borrows from its citizens, it has made the most solemnly binding commitment that an honest government can make. It has taken the people's substance for its own purposes and has promised to return the same with interest. They are entitled to their own again.

THE MOST insidious temptation faced by government is that of defrauding its citizens through some kind of repudiation of the public debt. This has taken many forms through the long centuries since rulers discovered the trick—currency debasement, outright repudiation, and general skulduggery of every sort whereby the people who had worked and saved to support the government were robbed by it. Adam Smith said that there was, even in his day (1776), no instance of a large public debt ever having been honestly and fairly paid. And the public debts with which he was familiar would not rate even as "peanuts" or "chickenfeed" today. They were only in millions, but ours is in billions, and we are approaching the stage of trillions.

In a practical sense, few persons can grasp the meaning of a million dollars, and no one can comprehend how much is a billion dollars. Yet our government has reached the stage where a billion dollars is only a white chip on the board—the minimum ante if one expects to stay in the game. And the Congressmen who vote a billion dollars for this or that purpose have absolutely no understanding of what this means in the "blood, sweat, and taxes" of the people.

The federal debt now stands at some $260 billion, a completely incomprehensible sum even to an astronomer. Yet this total is the number of dollars that the government has taken—or created—and spent in years past over and above the dollars taken out of current income in taxes.

The stupendous fact is that the federal government has created, and has committed itself to repay to someone, this perfectly enormous and incomprehensible sum. What does this mean? Does it mean anything? Does the federal government really intend to collect $260 billion from those who pay taxes and deliver it to those who own bonds?

For a time this issue can be dodged by semantic devices such as saying that we merely owe the debt to ourselves, or that by a sufficient growth of national production the debt will in time become relatively unimportant. These dodges, and all other tricks of national bookkeeping, cannot forever obscure the fact that the government spent X billions that were obtained from the savings of individuals and institutions or from an expansion of credit. The purpose of the spending will not then be material—whether war, relief, internal improvements, or whatever.

The choices are all unpleasant. Redemption would mean that for upwards of a century taxpayers, including bondholders, will be levied upon in order to repay bondholders. If the debt is to be carried perpetually at no more than 2½ per cent interest, it would mean a total tax burden for interest equal to the principal every 40 years. If the debt were to be scaled down or repudiated it would amount to robbery of those who originally loaned to the government, or their heirs.

No government should operate in this way. The purposes for

which government exists and the ends which it is created to serve, are those that fulfill such common needs of all as can best be met through the collective organization we know as government. These purposes must be paid for by the people as they go. If this rule is not rigorously followed, those who lend to government run the grave risk of not being fully reimbursed, because their very willingness to lend tempts government to borrow beyond its ability—or political willingness—to repay.

THE PUBLIC DEBT IS DEFERRED TAXATION

A public debt, honestly incurred with an intent to repay, is merely deferred taxation. The people are currently spared a tax burden which they must assume over the years to come. The case for this practice must always depend upon the relation between available tax resources and the public service obligations devolving upon the particular governmental unit. The federal government has less reason to borrow for any purpose than state or local governments because its tax resources are greatest of all. That it has done so to a degree so far beyond the borrowings of state and local governments is, *per se,* an indictment of federal fiscal management.

WE DEAL here only with debts that are to be repaid. Such debts are, evidently, only deferred taxation. They represent certain sums acquired by government for current spending—for whatever purpose is not now material—on a commitment to repay the same at a future time. Obviously, the only way that such a commitment can be honored is by levying taxes sufficient, over the period of the debt, to repay the principal and also to carry the interest as it falls due.

The only important question is: Has this ever been necessary for the federal government, in view of its plenary power of taxation? The only instance in which an affirmative answer might rightly be given is that of war. But even here the case is extremely doubtful. The real burden of war falls on the war generation, for it must endure whatever deprivations are involved in the diversion of current product to the war effort. Since the real deprivation is in the area of goods and services diverted from private to public consumption, it is always possible to siphon off enough private income to balance the account, provided the government—its administrators and legislators—have enough political wisdom and courage to impose the kinds and amounts of taxes that will accomplish this result. In the past they have lacked both the wisdom and the courage to do this, hence the immense public debt that now bears upon the people. This debt is, in large part, a result of the faulty financing methods of World War II.

The other purpose for which federal borrowing and spending are being urged currently is the so-called "investment" expenditures, those that are expected to return an income directly or that are assumed to expand general taxpaying capacity sufficiently to offset the debt. To these alleged justifications of borrowing the following brief answers are given:

First, government has no rightful warrant to enter fields of enterprise where income might be expected because it is thereby competing with its own taxpaying citizens.

Second, income allegedly realized from such ventures is usually a result of accounting that is manipulated to omit charges for many costs that a private enterprise must consider. Where allowance for such omissions is honestly made, there is no income in most cases.

Third, the collective judgment of the people as to the extent to which welfare is promoted by public spending can be relied upon if the bill is paid currently out of taxes. When the spending to promote the general welfare is financed out of loans, the people can exercise neither judgment nor control. The least, and the weakest, of all defenses of public borrowing is that it is done to promote the general welfare.

TAX POLICY

The key to a sound debt policy is a sound tax policy. Public debt is deferred taxation. Generally, it is better to pay all governmental costs out of current revenue than to borrow. The ability of the federal government to do this depends on the soundness of its tax system. The character of the taxation imposed influences alike the willingness of the people to pay taxes and, in extremity, their capacity to pay.

A SOUND tax system should have these objectives:

First, taxes should be so devised and levied as to impose the minimum restraint on the growth of the productive forces. Out of the battle of words over the relative importance of production versus consumption, this much seems clear: there would be some consumption even if the only production were what each of us could dig out of the ground with our bare hands. There could not possibly be the present high level of consumption unless the goods and services entering into it were produced. This production is due, first and foremost, to capital and technology. Labor is important, but how much could the 60,000,000 members of the employed labor force produce if, overnight, all capital, i.e., plant and equipment, were to be wiped out?

Second, all taxes are burdensome, but the manner in which the burden is laid will largely determine the degree of onerous effect involved. If it were possible to overcome prejudice and make the test, it would be found that many citizens would prefer to pay part of their tax as income is spent instead of paying so much of it as income is received. In England, where both income and excise taxes are very high, a recent public opinion poll disclosed that the first tax the people wanted reduced was the income tax, and that this was the last tax they wanted increased.

Third, taxes should be levied and collected for revenue purposes, and not to impose penalties or to manipulate the economy. The power to tax is so great, involving even the power to destroy, that its use should always be limited to serving the government's legitimate needs. The police powers and proper penalties imposed thereunder are the appropriate remedy for the violation of laws or the prevention of unsocial practices. It is a perversion of the taxing power to utilize it as a substitute for the police power.

The use of taxation to manipulate or influence the economy implies that someone—the person, department, or agency that makes the decisions for such use—knows better than anyone else what needs doing. There are no such supermen. A free economy advances by trial and error, but it advances steadily. The movement of a regimented economy—and use of the taxing power for manipulative purposes is regimentation—is determined by the pace set by the planners, and the direction of their particular bias, prejudice, or intelligence.

Fourth, the tax burden should be distributed as widely as possible among the citizens. There should be no large exempt groups or classes.

Fifth, a variety of taxes should be used. Too great reliance on any one tax is a threat to budgetary stability. Moreover, it would require tax rates so high as to interfere unduly, at some point or other, with the normal functioning and growth of the economy.

Sixth, since all taxes come out of income either as it is received or as it is spent, the tax system should be reasonably balanced between the levies on the receipt, and on the spending of income, respectively, to avoid excessive rates of tax on either production or consumption.

SPENDING POLICY

The key to a sound tax policy is a proper and sensible restraint with respect to public spending. Here is the original evil, the first cause, of bad financial management. Overspending leads to heavy taxes, and to gain a temporary respite from heavy tax burdens, resort is had to borrowing. Unrestrained debt financing eventually causes inflation and the end of that road is currency debasement, destruction of values, loss of faith in the government, and acceptance of the crackpot "isms" that flourish best amid poverty and despair.

CONTROL OF public spending is the central issue of sound, capable financial management. It can be achieved only by holding fast to two guiding principles:

First, the truly essential services of government, the performance of which is the prime justification for the existence of government, are relatively few in number. The cost of these essential services would never be great. Many fringe and nonessential services have been added and it is the cost of these, rather than of the essential services, that breaks taxpayers' backs and leads to mountains of debt.

Second, the whole cost of government should be paid out of current revenue.

The best way of determining what services, and how much of any service, government is to render is to present the bill for these services to the people every year. This is expressed in the constitutional concept that sovereignty inheres in the people because they control the purse strings. But they have this control only to the extent that they insist on paying the bills currently. When escape is offered, or sought, by postponement through borrowing they have foregone their control and they later have no choice, judgment, or discretion as to payment.

A seductive fiscal doctrine is that the national budget need not be balanced every year, but only over the business cycle.

That is, let deficits occur in some years and accumulate sur-pluses in other years to redeem the debt thus incurred. This scheme is a snare and a delusion. It presumes better forecast-ing than any statistical agency can do in predicting the begin-ning, duration, and termination of economic cycles. It ignores the practical political disposition to let the debt accumulate instead of redeeming it, while meantime spending the surplus revenues for enlarged public benefits. It would result in a steady growth of the public debt with all of the eventual menace to currency stability that debt increase involves.

Candidates for public office face a strong temptation to promise benefits if elected. Oddly enough, these promises sometimes get votes, even among those who know they will pay higher taxes if the promises are carried out. An effective cure for promises of this sort would be a requirement that every appropriation bill show precisely how the money it proposes to spend is to be raised, whether from existing taxes, new taxes, or higher rates of tax.

EFFICIENCY AND ECONOMY

The test of good government is simple—it is the test of economical and efficient administration. Government has no resources of its own. All that it has is taken, in some way, from the people. Hence, all government is, in es-sence, a stewardship, a holding, use, and application of the people's resources in trust for the faithful performance of those services and functions which the people have delegated to government. Any failure to be efficient and economical is a betrayal of a public trust. As Benjamin Franklin said, "No revenue is sufficient without economy."

THE TERMS "economy" and "efficiency" have been much mis-used but they are none the less valid and vital as tests of the competence of public administration. It is not uncommon to encounter shocking examples of public waste and inefficiency, to which the reaction of the average person always is that any private business operated in such a manner would shortly be in bankruptcy.

When taxes are paid something—i.e., income—which is a prized possession of the taxpayer while in his hands, passes into public control where there is no sense of personal ownership. Public funds belong to no one because they belong to all. It is understandable that there should be a less sensitive and responsible attitude toward such funds than there is toward one's own private income or wealth.

But to understand this attitude is not to condone it. The citizens have severally and individually lost control of the income that they have paid as taxes, but they have not lost their right to a competent stewardship by their government. Without the energy, industry, initiative, and other economic and moral qualities of the people, the government's revenues would be small regardless of the drastic measures it might apply. It is the people's money that government spends, for it has nothing of its own to spend. Private trustees are not permitted to play fast and loose with the funds committed to their care. "A public office is a public trust," it has been said, and with complete truth.

The betrayal of public trust seldom occurs through defalcation. Its most common form is waste, supported by all the formalities of appropriation and due process made and prescribed for paying out public funds. More serious than theft is the inclination to use, or to authorize the use of, public funds for purposes more in the interest of partisan advantage than genuinely in the public interest. When this temptation wins out, considerations of economy and efficiency will already have been discarded, for these principles have significance only as the general public good is involved.

Part II

THE STATE, THE PARTY, AND THE PEOPLE

THE PRESENT section deals with some general principles involving the relationship between a political party and the people, on one hand, and between the party and the state, on the other. The preceding essays have shown that preservation of the essential basis of freedom, which is the *right* to own, depends on the permanence and stability of government, and that these, in turn, depend on the proper management of the public finances. A bankrupt government cannot protect anybody, even itself.

In the discussion that follows, the significance of the political party is emphasized. The state, as such, is an abstraction. Its visible and responsible agent is what we call "the government," but the active, moving power in the government at any given time is the political party that happens then to be in control. In a free, democratic society, this control will have been acquired with the consent of the people.

The discussion of the responsibility that devolves upon a political party as it assumes the administrative task of operating the affairs of state is presented from the point of view that the people must support and control the government, rather than be supported and controlled by it.

THE POLITICAL PARTY SYSTEM

The American constitutional system is based on the premise that sovereignty inheres in the people. The Constitution recognizes and declares that the people have agreed to establish a government which shall perform certain duties, services, and functions for them. It does not fully prescribe, however, the procedure whereby the people shall express their sovereignty to these particular ends beyond certain provisions relating to elections.

But elections presuppose political parties and the whole machinery of determining policies, selecting candidates for the various offices, and managing political campaigns. The political party is, therefore, an important institution for the realization of our way of life, and upon its proper functioning depends the success with which the will of the people is expressed as public policy.

THROUGHOUT the national history the American people have been exceedingly fortunate in that there have always been only two major political parties. The original cleavage in political views involved the difference between a broad and a strict construction of the powers delegated to the federal government by the Constitution. Despite the various changes of party labels and party attitudes, this is still the basic point of opposition in political viewpoints.

The two-party system is the best of all arrangements. Where there is only one party, as in dictator countries, the election process degenerates into a fraudulent and farcical parody on the genuine free expression of the popular will. Where there are numerous parties, no one of them is likely to have sufficient electoral support to form a responsible government and the execution of the popular will is at the mercy of ever-changing combinations or "blocs." The result is continual confusion, irresponsibility, and the absence of consistent policy.

The integrity of the two-party system in the United States is threatened today by the tendency of certain economic groups to engage in political action, as groups. The avowed aim is to mold public policy into patterns that will directly enhance the economic advantage of these groups and of their individual members, regardless of the consequences of such action for the public interest as a whole. Candidates for office are supported or opposed solely on the basis of their attitude toward the specific measures demanded by these pressure groups, and with no regard or concern for the qualifications of these candidates to deal with any or all other matters of national importance, well-being, or security.

This trend must be checked if a decay of the two-party system is to be averted. The temptation to cater to the demands of special interest groups must be resisted. A great obligation rests on those who write party platforms, who manage political parties, and who aspire to office under the aegis of their chosen party. This obligation is to assure government of, for, and by the people, and not government as the special franchise of some pressure group.

CONSTITUTIONAL CHECKS AND BALANCES

A central and most difficult problem that confronts every free society is this: How to create a government that is strong enough to perform the duties and services required of it and at the same time to prevent that government from gaining such power and control as to jeopardize personal liberties and free institutions.

THE FOUNDING FATHERS were fully aware of this problem. They devised a solution that has been acclaimed as ingenious and efficacious. It was the system of checks and balances, whereby the three co-ordinate branches of the government—legislative, executive, and judicial—were respectively given certain powers, in the exercise of which each would be a check on the others and a counterweight against assumption of undue influence or authority by any of them.

This solution has not always worked as well as its authors expected it would. During the past generation the three branches of the federal government have collaborated in an expansion of the federal power and authority. There have been neither checks nor balances. Wars, and the threat of war, have more than once induced a delegation of extraordinary powers to the federal government. By and large these powers have been relinquished or stripped away after the emergency has passed, but the question that gives every thoughtful citizen concern is: Will this always happen? Or will more of these powers be kept, as some of them have been held after each previous emergency, until at last government has all the power and the individual has none of his liberties?

If these citizens, and all citizens, realized that the answer to their question lies in the vitality and integrity of their political parties then, while their concern would still be warranted, they would at least understand how to do something about it.

The explanation is that what we usually think of as "the government" is a political party in action. The President and the members of Congress in office have been elected as the candidates of a party. The policies that they express in legislative and administrative action are, or should be, those for which the party stands. Where there is lack of party integrity, there can be betrayal of the people. A significant test of party integrity is the sincerity of devotion, after election, to the pre-election promises and commitments.

Under the system of majority rule, one party or the other must always be the loser in any election. This need not diminish its stature or its influence. Elections occur periodically. Since the losing party always aspires to become the party in power, its best chance to realize this hope—or ambition—would appear to be in an adequate and convincing demonstration of statesmanship in opposition.

FUNCTIONS OF A POLITICAL PARTY

The functions of a political party are these: first, to provide an organized body of political doctrine—a platform—to serve as a rallying point for all citizens who hold certain views with respect to the duties and responsibilities which they believe the government should assume and discharge; second, to supply active leadership for its members and supporters to the end that these views may be realized and effectuated in public policy; third, to maintain a stern sense of responsibility for fulfilling the commitments that have been made to the party members and to the country.

THESE THREE aspects of the function of a political party have seldom had equal recognition and emphasis. In particular, disregard of the third point—maintenance of a stern and honest sense of responsibility for fulfilling the commitments made in the party platform—has been largely responsible for the ill repute into which party platforms have fallen. These documents have not been taken seriously as the guide to the course of policy to be followed, and hence have too often been regarded as intended for pre-election consumption only. It has therefore too often happened that some platform promises have been the more extravagant because there was never an intention of performance.

A significant contributory factor to the decline of party prestige has been the lack of responsibility among party leaders for holding the rank and file of the membership to the line of the policy—or platform—statement. Doing this does not involve thought control or dictatorship by party leaders. It does mean that, after having been elected on the basis of certain principles and policies, the party membership should remember and abide by them. For one thing, stricter party responsibility and discipline of this sort would keep many foolish things out of the platform. As a document it would show more exactly just what the party stood for, and the duty of living up to it would be more easily met.

Enhancement of party rating in the sight and thought of the people can be definitely achieved by the honesty and sincerity shown both in writing the platform and in standing on it afterward. This is true, whether the party in question be in the majority or in the minority. The proof of capacity to take over the government and operate it is in the statesmanship displayed. Any minority party must build its proof by the quality and caliber of its statecraft in opposition.

PLATFORM OR CANDIDATE

In the practical sense, our political contests are struggles for offices and for the material and intangible rewards connected with officeholding. From this standpoint there is little case for emphasis on party platforms and political principles. But in the fundamental, as distinguished from the practical, sense, the principles for which a party stands are more important than its candidates. The main issue that should divide parties is not whether to elect A and B rather than X and Y, but rather the fundamental question: What shall government do? How far shall its activities, authority, and burden extend?

THIS IS more than a statement of the obvious contrast between practical politics and political idealism. It is a reminder that there is more to governing than offices and the emoluments of office. The attention and effort of the candidates and party members who enter the hot, dusty arena of political campaigning are directed at capturing the offices. But the too-frequent acceptance of the view that the spoils belong to the victors confirms the proposition that where the principal matter considered to be important is whether one or another group of candidates shall occupy offices, dispense favors and patronage, reward supporters and penalize opponents in making appointments, awarding contracts, etc., the platform is of minor importance, or none at all.

There is, unavoidably, more to governing than patronage, particularly at the national level. Even those who are elected to national office with no higher vision than that of sharing the spoils are forced to make decisions on great issues. These decisions will inevitably influence the direction the government takes, whether or not the persons making them realize it. Unless there is an intelligible, consistent party doctrine and a strong sense of party responsibility for the application of this doctrine in conducting public affairs, decisions of grave import are likely to be made at haphazard.

In shaping a party platform to express policy with regard to the central political issue, namely, the character of government functions and the scope of government powers, the most logical dividing line is that between a narrow and a broad interpretation. Other terms have been used, such as "left" and "right," "conservative" and "radical," and so on. The precise terms used do not greatly matter for some of them have been used with different meanings from one period to another. It is important, however, to understand the difference in objective, to know that in one direction there is a limitation of governmental powers, authority, and cost, while in the other direction there is a continual expansion of governmental powers, authority, and cost.

Here is, or should be, the basic cleavage between party principles and doctrines. If we assume that all men desire freedom, then the question is: In what direction is freedom found? Toward the "right" or the "left"? Toward conservatism or radicalism? Party platforms should give and justify answers. It is in this respect that the platform is more important than the candidate.

THE INDEPENDENT VOTER

In an important sense, the independent voter is the decisive element in American politics. He is courted by both parties and his decisions are often controlling in close elec-

tion counts. The number of such voters is large, though
not exactly known. A problem that vexes all party managers is: Why so many independents and what can be
done to reduce the number?

THE EXPLANATION of the independent voter seems fairly simple. It is that he is not satisfied, intellectually or emotionally
or in some other way, with the program of either party. He
therefore prefers and insists upon keeping aloof from party
alignment and commitment.

Realism compels recognition of the fact that no one program
or platform can fully satisfy the aims and aspirations of the
entire electorate. There is room, as there should be, for honest
differences of opinion. The important thing, in building party
platforms, is to do the job in such a spirit of genuine concern
for the public good as to carry conviction to those who have
regarded themselves as independents.

More than this, it is important to educate the voters in the
fundamentals of the American Way and how a particular program or platform proposes to preserve and strengthen it. The
often-heard cynical comment, "That's just politics," should
cease to be an appropriate observation. After all, "playing
politics" implies a degree of indifference to, or ignorance of,
fundamentally honest principles of government and economics
that is dangerous and appalling, if true.

A political platform must therefore be specific, not general.
It must be direct, not evasive. It must hold the general good
of all above the particular advantage of some. It must carry in
its words the conviction of a high sense of responsibility for
the fate of the nation and the leading party members must
never swerve from this conviction.

A party that writes such a platform and follows through
on it after election will shortly convert independents into en-
thusiastic party members. Remember, they are independent

more because they await signs of competent leadership than because they are merely cantankerous.

PRINCIPLE VERSUS EXPEDIENCY

The sorest temptation that confronts party managers and party platform makers is that of temporizing with principle in order to get votes. Under this pressure the typical party platform becomes a conglomeration of vote-seeking promises that offer something for the aged, for the farmers, for labor, and a little, sometimes, for business. Why not, for a change, and one that might be surprisingly welcome to all of these groups, write a platform that will show how each benefit or favor has its cost and that the only way to have the benefit is to pay the cost?

A great service will be rendered by the party that shows clearly what is the end of the road of more and more government, what it will cost to get there, and what it will be like when we shall have arrived. It should also be shown where the road of less government leads, what must be given up if we take it, and what will be at the end. Socialism and freedom are wholly incompatible. There is still time to make the choice, and our political parties have a heavy responsibility for helping the people to make it.

THE PRACTICE of offering promises for votes is as old as the art of politics. Superficially, it would appear that the credulity of voters far exceeds their memory. Remembrance should warn them that more such promises are broken than kept. And ordinary common sense should advise them that any deliveries on promises must somehow be paid for. Nevertheless, it continues to be good vote-getting technique to promise extravagantly.

The reason for this is that credulity has been fostered by deception. Any party or candidate can dispel the deception with plain speaking about plain truths. Here are some examples of such plain truths.

First, government has no resources of its own. All it has it has taken from the people. Therefore, it really has nothing to lend, to give away, or to use in any way to support the people. It is always their money that government is paying them, or giving them, or spending to provide benefits.

Second, nothing that government does by spending, lending, or giving, is costless. The cost may be concealed from all for a time, as when it is met by loans instead of taxes. It may be concealed from some for quite a time, as when taxes on certain groups or sections are used to pay special benefits to other groups or sections. Nevertheless, the costs are there and will fall, eventually, one way or another, on all.

Third, all government benefits, aids, and subsidies, or largess in any form, lead to more government control and authority. This is both logical and inevitable. The price of complete support by government is complete surrender to the terms set by the supporting government.

Fourth, the end of the road traveled by ever-expanding government is socialism. This is the final installment of the price to be paid for tolerating the step by step advance of more government. It is sheer sophistry to argue that because none of the separate steps, by itself, has brought us to socialism, therefore each separate step may be taken though it be admittedly socialistic. One brick does not make a wall, but enough bricks laid up together do make a wall.

PLATFORM INTEGRITY

The highest test of party worthiness to govern is that of the general policy attitude that is displayed while in power. We have said more than once in these pages that the party in power *is* the government in action. And while it is in power, while it is, in effect, the visible and operating government, it faces a constant succession of choices all of which are reducible to the difference between honor and dishonor. That is to say, the party in power must continually balance the permanent general good against temporary partisan advantage. As the agent and personification of government, its acts must scrupulously avoid taint of special favor or unwarranted penalty. The weakest of all reasons for any government—i.e., party-in-power—policy is that it is politically necessary and expedient. This is the path of dishonor for those to whose care have been entrusted the fortunes and the destiny of any nation.

A HIGH STANDARD of party and individual rectitude has been set here. But how can any lower standard be established? All of the citizens are, in a very real sense, at the mercy of the government, which means that they are at the mercy of the party that happens, at any given time, to be the active agent of the abstraction called "the government." The party has no resources of its own, and no powers of action other than those that have been vested in it by the suffrages of a majority of the voting electorate. What we are saying here is that it is a dishonorable betrayal of the people's trust to use these powers, or to apply any part of the entrusted resources, to partisan or selfish ends. There can be only one honorable guide, which is that of the most enlightened service of the public interest and good as a whole.

This point has always deserved emphasis because of the long-accepted view that public office is a means of personal and party aggrandizement. The point is particularly important because of the low state of political morality that has developed as disregard of the general public good has more completely permeated party policy.

It is unnecessary to repeat well-known details of the degree to which those in high position and their hangers-on have utilized their connections to reap private, personal gains and to promote the party advantage. There must be a thorough house cleaning of such practices. The taxes that the people pay to support the government must be conserved for public purposes. What is proposed here is a return to the concept so well stated by more than one of the able statesmen of an earlier generation, that a public office is a public trust, not a means of private, personal gain.

MORE GOVERNMENT, OR LESS?

Both historically and in the present, the conflict of interests and ideologies which may be summarily stated as the issue of less government or more government, really involves the status of the individual. His freedom and his rights would suffer equally if there were no government or if there were all-powerful government. There is little likelihood that any modern society will deliberately revert to the chaos of no government, although this has happened for brief periods under the stress of revolution or complete military disaster. There is a serious danger, however, that by making one concession after another, a nation of people who really prefer individual freedom may discover that they have finally yielded everything to an all-powerful government.

THE HISTORY of government in all ages is the record of the individual versus the state. During the greater part of this record, the state has been all-powerful and all-important. Here in the United States men have realized a greater degree of freedom than was ever achieved anywhere else, at any time. During the first century and a quarter there was sharp contest over less or more government, and between federalism and states' rights. At no time, however, was the area of controversy broad enough to involve serious jeopardy for individual freedom and the American way of life. A good measure of the extent of this controversial area is the cost of government, for it is self-evident that the functions and authority of government are indicated by their costs. Prior to World War I, total federal spending was never as much as $1 billion a year, and the cost of all government—federal, state, and local—did not absorb more than 5 to 6 per cent of the national income.

The two world wars caused a large increase of costs and a permanent increase of the federal bureaucracy. Government now requires more than 30 per cent of a much larger national income. The inflationary financing used in both wars depreciated the currency, expanded money incomes, and accumulated an immense public debt.

Similar problems were met and dealt with after the Civil War. We could have dealt with the wastes, the currency depreciation, the debt, and the bureaucratic expansion produced by the two world wars. But this is not all.

There has developed over the past 40 years, and with special intensity over the past 20 years, another menace to individual freedom and the American Way that is more dangerous by far than taxes and currency depreciation because it is concealed beneath a whitened exterior of free benefits, governmental grants and subsidies, and other devices whereby freedom is being exchanged for security. The core of this insidious doctrine is that government can and should support the people; that government support is a right; and that the cost of such support is of no consequence since, even if debt must be issued to provide it, the debt is merely owed to ourselves.

Again the issue is clear. Are we to inch our way into a condition in which government provides everything, controls everything, owns everything, and meanwhile trade our freedom for the dubious security of a socialist, police state? Or are we to take a firm stand against this easy descent into the economic underworld? Whichever way we go, our action will be through a political party.

FREEDOM THROUGH LESS GOVERNMENT

The program or platform to be developed here is designed for a political party that is prepared to accept and stand on the principle that the services, powers, and cost of government must alike be restricted and reduced if individual freedom and rights are to be preserved. A corollary of this principle is that the regimentation and socialization that have been so manifest in this country will lead eventually to the completely authoritarian, socialized state if the trend in that direction is not halted. A political party cannot exist and function effectively without broad popular support. It is believed that a clear, straightforward declaration of policies, all of which are based upon and are relevant to the basic proposition that the individual is more significant than the state, will have overwhelming popular support.

THE REASONS for a party platform based on the principle that the powers and cost of government must be reduced should be fairly clear. They include, among others, the following points of vital importance to every citizen:

First, the expansion of the powers and authority of government necessarily means a curtailment of individual freedom. All government dealings and operations affect, in one way or another, the business, or the income, or the well-being, of persons. As the area occupied by government expands, that remaining to be occupied by individuals contracts. Two bodies cannot occupy the same space at the same time.

Second, governmental expansion costs money and this means heavier taxes. For a time the expansion can be financed by higher taxes on large incomes and estates, but these sources of revenue do not last, as has been demonstrated in socialist England. Eventually, the cost of the program must fall on everyone. As the governmental bureaucracy grows in size it becomes progressively more wasteful and hence more costly.

The multiple overlapping of federal agencies that has already occurred in our short journey into socialization has become a national scandal, but it is only a natural product of public operations conducted by drawing on that perpetual fountain, the taxpayers' pocketbook.

Third, as the area of wasteful government expands and the areas available to prudent individual operation contract, a point is reached at which the citizens cannot carry the load. In air-flight parlance this is the "point of no return." Unless we can turn back before this point is reached, there will be no choice other than complete socialization.

The only safe conclusion, and the only safe platform for a political party dedicated to individual freedom and the American way of life is to reject further expansion of governmental powers and cost, and to show the way to a real salvation of the principles and values for which we are willing to fight, and if necessary, to die.

Part III

THE PLATFORM

Section 1

THE ROAD TO LESS GOVERNMENT

THE PRECEDING Part II outlines a philosophy of party policy
and action. The essence of this philosophy is:

1. In the age-old conflict of man versus the state, this platform champions man, the individual.

2. The preservation of individual rights demands an unceas-
ing fight against the encroachments of government upon these
rights.

3. A political party in power, being for the time government
in action and therefore the visible, responsible representative
of the state, must demonstrate the sincerity and integrity of its
fight for the individual by the extent to which it is prepared
to curb the authority of the state. The expansion and encroachment whereby the area of individual rights has been diminished and the prospect of enduring individual freedom has
been darkened, have occurred through the acts and with the
consent of political parties.

A party that intends to stand for more individual freedom
must insist that some governmental power be relinquished.
It must cut down rather than increase further the cost and
burden of government. It must substitute skilled leadership
for paternalistic support.

There would remain, even after these changes, a proper area
of public functions large enough to satisfy the legitimate ambi-
tions of office seekers and to strain to the utmost their administrative competence.

33

"BRING GOVERNMENT BACK HOME"

The first step in reducing the size, power, and cost of the federal government is to reach agreement on the services and functions that it should perform. Thus will be provided a basis for discovering the operations now being conducted that are not properly governmental activities at all, and those other operations which, if found to be properly within the area of public functions, should be transferred to other jurisdictions, such as the states or their local units. Much of the recent expansion of the federal government has been at the expense of the states, both with respect to the absorption of functions that the states can and should perform, and also with respect to the parallel absorption of tax resources.

THE FEDERAL GOVERNMENT is too big. It is so big that it cannot be managed efficiently by any man or group of men. Because of this immense size the burden of its cost is a greater load than the economy can carry and remain prosperous. The performance of unnecessary, or of duplicating, services by a host of superfluous personnel does not add to the product of the national economy, although the statisticians include government spending in the over-all total of gross national product. It is time to recognize that government spending is not synonymous with productivity, but rather, that it is a dead weight on the productive forces when it goes beyond the cost of the truly needed, constructive services and functions for which government exists.

The remedy for this situation is to reduce the size, power, and cost of the federal government. A program to achieve this end will involve surgery but there are times when the knife must be used to save the patient. However, in this case the loss will be excess fat rather than blood. The present writer has outlined at various times over the past decade the essential steps that will be required. These steps may be summarized as follows:

1. Curtailment of the scope and burden of the federal government by:
   a. Elimination of services, notably those inaugurated under depression or other emergency conditions which have now terminated.
   b. Return to the states of various functions and services which can and should be handled by them.
   c. Introduction of economy measures such as reorganization of departments, and improved standards of departmental and agency management.
2. A realignment of taxation methods whereby the states may acquire the financial resources necessary to perform the services that may be assigned to them without the infliction of excessive tax burdens on the people.

Both aspects of the problem must be considered together. The subject of overlapping or duplicate taxation by federal and state governments has received attention off and on over the last fifteen years. It has virtually always been approached in these discussions as if it were separable from the allocation of service responsibilities. These matters are not separable and no plan of revenue allocation can succeed unless it is accompanied by a parallel program of changes in the distribution of functions. By the same token, no proposal to shift important administrative tasks from federal to state jurisdiction can succeed without at the same time providing that the states shall have greater revenue resources for their own use.

An examination of the things that the federal government is now doing discloses three areas of operation that are not properly governmental functions at all. One involves lending, a second involves giving, and a third involves business competition with its citizens. Elimination of these improper activities is a first, and necessary, step toward reducing the size and cost of government.

FEDERAL LENDING

The first of the fields of federal operation that should be eliminated is lending. This is not a proper governmental function in any sense. Collateral to this activity is the guarantee of loans and various forms of loan insurance.

The making of loans implies that the lender possesses assets which can be advanced to the borrower. But the government has no assets of its own. Everything that it has or can get must first come from the people. By what right or prerogative does the government take the people's money and lend it?

LENDING IS NOT a proper function of government because government has nothing to lend. Any funds that are passed out as loans must first be taken from the people in taxes, or be obtained by the government's own borrowing. Lending always involves some degree of risk, however secure the borrower's prospects may appear. A loan by government means that it is willing to risk the taxpayers' money in ways, or on terms, that these taxpayers themselves might not consider prudent. If the citizens, individually or through their own private lending institutions, are not willing to take the risk of a particular loan, there can be no defense of government's action in assuming that risk in their stead, with their money.

Guarantee and insurance of loans fall into the same category. The fact that such ultimate protection is deemed necessary indicates an element of risk that private lenders are not willing to assume. The federal guarantee does make mortgages and other debt paper salable, that might not otherwise be floated. But the basic proposition remains the same. It is that government has no right to assume risks with the people's funds, or with their ultimate obligation to pay taxes in the case of guarantees, that they would not assume on their own initiative.

The federal credit program has now attained enormous proportions. The budget estimates for the fiscal year 1953 show a total credit authority, as of June 30, 1953, of $71,162 million, against which, by that time, the total charges will amount to $57,421 million. These are utterly fantastic figures.

As of June 30, 1951, the total loans of all insured commercial banks were only $54,300 million.

All federal lending should be terminated. The capacity of private institutions to supply all credit for which there is a demonstrable need and an adequate security is such that there can be no case for continued government competition in this field. The numerous federal lending agencies should be consolidated into a small number to operate henceforth only to collect outstanding loans under contracts already made. When this task is finished the collecting agencies should be liquidated.

GRANTS-IN-AID

The second area of operation in which government has no proper place is giving money away. It does this through grants and subsidies. Grants are made to public units such as the states and their subdivisions, and subsidies are the gifts made to individuals or private groups. Having nothing of its own to give, government first takes money from the people, or some of the people, and then distributes it to others as grants or subsidies. Through this enforced philanthropy there has been built up great prestige and control under the cloak of the illusion that the gifts are costless. Federal money is regarded by the beneficiaries as free money.

THE ANNUAL REPORTS of the Secretary of the Treasury show that federal grants to the states have increased from $35 million in 1920 to $2,281 million in 1951. During the 1920's these grants comprised no more than 5 per cent of state tax collections from their own resources. In 1940 this percentage had risen to 17.3, and in 1950 it was 28.2 per cent. The budget estimate of the grand total for the fiscal year 1953 is more than $3 billion, an amount that will be at least one-third as much as the states themselves are collecting.

This record means a dangerous increase of state dependency

on federal bounty. It must always be understood that the money handed out is not free, or costless. Yet so strongly entrenched is the illusion that it is burdenless that even responsible state and local officials sometimes yield to the spell.

The great shift of tax power from the states to the federal government over the past 20 years has reduced state capacity to pay the costs of state and local government out of tax resources available to them and thus has made the apparent case for grants stronger. And as the total of the grants rose, higher federal taxes were required to pay them. If the grant policy is allowed to continue and expand, the vicious circle of federal tax squeeze and greater state dependency will eventually wreck the sovereignty of the states. Once they become so dependent on federal support that it cannot be refused, their capacity to resist federal domination will be gone. Elimination of state independence and resistance is an essential prelude to the establishment of a national socialist regime. The grant system is a powerful instrument for this elimination.

The federal grant to the states is wrong in principle and illusory as an enduring form of tax relief. It is wrong because it always involves some degree of federal control over the service or activity for which the grant is given. And as the controls multiply the right and ability of the states to make their own decisions are diminished.

The federal grant is an illusion, for the money given to the states must first be collected from the people. If it be urged that the grant is justifiable as a means of transferring wealth and income from one section of the country to another, the answer is that no section would for long provide even a superficial case for such aid if the burden of federal taxes and federal regulation were sufficiently lightened. There is no part of the United States that is not capable of great growth and development through private enterprise and investment. The reduction of federal burdens will release the funds necessary for this investment and provide the incentive for their use. No arbitrary transfers by government are needed.

The whole grant policy should be eliminated as rapidly as existing commitments can be liquidated. Under a sound re-allocation of tax resources between federal and state governments the states would be able to obtain their own revenues to support their own services. Being thus put on their own, the states might not severally adopt all of the programs now supported by federal grants. This should be their privilege. A local judgment, in some cases, would be more realistic as to the need and value of the service than one formulated by the federal government and "sold" to the states with the lure of a grant-in-aid.

SUBSIDIES

In addition to giving money to the states, under the high-sounding title of "grants-in-aid," the federal government also operates an extensive program of giving money away to individuals and groups. This kind of public philanthropy with the funds of private citizens is known as a "subsidy."

Such gifts are usually introduced in periods of economic distress. Experience shows, however, that they are not canceled when the circumstances change. Rather, they tend to become more strongly entrenched and more costly, for two reasons: first, if there is a genuinely bad or un-desirable economic situation, the subsidy does not cure it nor does it provide an incentive to those affected to better their own condition; and second, for whatever reason inaugurated, these gifts speedily become vested rights. The proponents are more insistent, more articulate, even more threatening, than the opponents. This is not strange for the opponents have usually been the taxpayers, who are the most disunited, inarticulate, meek, and long-suffering group in any society.

WE DEAL here with some of the most difficult and elusive aspects of governmental action. They involve broad issues of policy in the large area of business and economic activities. It is taken for granted here that the maximum degree of individual and collective well-being will be attained when there is the fullest and freest expression of the driving forces which motivate individuals to work, to produce, to save, and invest. Under this assumption where and why should government interfere with subsidies, whether open or concealed?

The answer is that no broad justification of subsidies can be given. No economic pursuit can be justified if its result, in terms of product, cannot be sold to consumers at a price that will cover costs plus some sort of return to those who have supplied the capital. Why, then, should government take from citizens who are individually unwilling to buy the product of a given concern or industry at reasonable or adequate prices in the open market a portion of their respective incomes and deliver it to the business units that are unable to muster enough market support to stay afloat?

This is what a subsidy always means. It is a payment out of public revenues which are derived through taxation from citizens generally, to some select or favored industry or group. It is, by the same token, an admission that the product or service of this favored industry or group is not sufficiently valued by consumers in a competitive market to bring a return adequate to cover costs and a fair yield on capital.

Frankly, this is not the way to promote sound national economic growth. In the vast, complex process of production and consumption there is, or should be, a continual weeding out of the unfit. The millions of workers and investors get income for their respective contributions to production. In a free society they may spend this income as suits their need or fancy, or they may save and invest it. Whole industries may rise or fall according to the shifting preference of consumers.

Those who fail to keep touch with these shifting preferences are, economically, the unfit. Government subsidies are a way of arbitrarily redirecting consumer preferences and expenditure so that the economically unfit are kept afloat, in contradiction of the course of nature and economic fact.

SUBSIDIES FOR NATIONAL DEFENSE

The one point at which a case for subsidy can be made is in connection with production for national defense. This is because the ordinary standards of value, price, cost, and demand that operate in a free, peacetime market are not applicable to an urgent military situation. It is necessary, however, to keep a tight rein here to prevent a general diffusion of subsidy payments under the loose pretext that in modern, total war, virtually everything that is produced is likely to be useful for defense. The primary test should always be that the subsidy becomes necessary, even for defense purposes, only after a demonstration that there will not be adequate production under the operation of ordinary market forces and conditions. Even so, the extent of the subsidy should be limited to the amount necessary to supplement the customary private production.

Provision for adequate and effective national defense is a major federal obligation. This requires materials and equipment as well as personnel. Ordinarily, the many kinds of goods needed to equip and supply the armed forces are being made, or can readily be made, by private business concerns. Where retooling or other conversion steps are necessary, the contract terms should cover the expense involved.

There are certain areas of production, however, in which the military need, in the event of intensive rearming or outright war, will be much greater than the ordinary peacetime demand for the product. Where its character is such as to require highly specialized skills and a basic foundation of management and organization, it may be necessary to subsidize the industry rather than assume the risk of disintegration through lack of a sufficient private market.

Two examples are the aircraft industry and the shipbuilding industry. Both aircraft and ships are used in much larger volume in war than in the ordinary commerce of peace. In each case the construction process is long and complicated, involving a substantial number of workers and a wide variety of skills. Particularly in the case of aircraft is it essential that there be continued research, experimentation, and development based on the newest findings.

In view of these considerations, there should be maintained, for both industries, the elements of management organization and technical skills as a base upon which there could be rapid expansion into large production in the event of emergency. The basic organization thus maintained would probably be larger than would be required to turn out all the aircraft, or ships, that could profitably be used during peace. The subsidy would be the cost involved in excess of the ordinary business earnings from the continuing civilian business. Such a subsidy would be properly a part of the military budget.

There is less case for subsidizing exploration for scarce metals and minerals. Such exploration is likely to proceed anyway, and if discoveries are made the depletion allowances of the tax laws are designed to provide funds for further exploration and development. Stockpiling is a better solution. This cost is now treated as part of the defense budget.

AGRICULTURAL SUBSIDIES

One of the most costly, and also the most indefensible, of the federal subsidies is that paid to favored segments of agriculture. The practice of direct subsidy payments to farmers was introduced during the 1930's on a large scale, following several years of active but unproductive political agitation during the later 1920's. The purpose of this policy was the economic relief of agriculture, and in the minds of many this objective provided a complete justification.

Economic distress was widespread during the depression of the early 1930's. Federal action of various kinds was supported at the time on the ground that suffering should not be tolerated anywhere while the power and the capacity to prevent it existed. This logic carried over into the farm program.

Actually, however, the economic distress of the farmers was of an entirely different order from that of the unemployed in the cities. The farm problem was an excess of fixed capital charges in the face of declining farm income. The heavy capital charges were a direct product of the immense farm mortgage debt that had been created. The unwisdom of having assumed this debt during the speculative years of the first World War and immediately thereafter mattered little when the foreclosure actions piled up in the depression.

Even if the agricultural subsidy program were justifiable as a relief measure, the case for it disappeared when the need for relief passed. That need has passed long since. Yet the agricultural subsidy program is more solidly entrenched, and its cost is greater than ever. Its economic unwisdom and unsoundness are also greater than ever.

THE CRISIS in agriculture that led to the inauguration and expansion of federal subsidies was of an entirely different order than the crisis of employment and income which led to the development of the various federal relief plans and relief agencies. The latter were, fundamentally, a result of deficiency of income and work from which to provide necessary food, clothing, and shelter for men, women, and children. On the other hand, there was no shortage of food and shelter for the farm population. In fact, had there not been an adequate food supply, no federal appropriation, however large, could have provided it except by importation.

The agricultural crisis was essentially a capital investment crisis. In this respect agriculture was in no greatly different position than nonfarm business, for there were enormous shrinkages of capital values and a great increase of business failures, throughout the American economy. The farm crisis was, perhaps, the more easily dramatized because mortgage foreclosure has always been a vivid way of portraying the tragedy of the loss of savings, of equity values, and of a way of life for the dispossessed. No comparable vividness can be injected into the failure of a business corporation that wipes out the equity of the stockholders, although the tragedy is as complete in the one case as in the other.

The source and character of the agricultural capital crisis can best be shown by statistics. The following tabulation shows, for the years 1916–1930 inclusive, the BLS index of the price of farm products, the estimated income from agriculture, and the farm mortgage debt outstanding:

Year	BLS Farm Product Price Index (1926 = 100)	Income from Agriculture (Billions)	Farm Mortgage Debt (Billions)
1916	84.4	$ 7.1	$ 5.8
1917	129.0	9.5	6.5
1918	128.0	11.5	7.1
1919	157.6	12.7	8.4
1920	150.7	10.6	10.2
1921	88.4	7.7	10.7
1922	93.8	7.0	10.8
1923	98.6	7.9	10.7
1924	100.0	8.5	9.9
1925	109.8	9.0	9.7
1926	100.0	8.6	9.7
1927	99.4	8.6	9.8
1928	105.9	8.8	9.8
1929	104.9	8.7	9.6
1930	88.3	6.8	9.4

Source: *Statistical Supplement to the Statistical Abstract of the U.S. Department of Commerce.*

The sequence from cause to effect is plain. The rapid rise in the price of farm products during and immediately after the first World War produced an equally startling rise in farm income, and a wholly unwarranted inflation in the prices of farm land. Farm mortgage debt at its peak in 1922 was almost double the total in 1916. The bottom fell out of farm product prices with the restoration of agriculture in Europe after the war and with the expanded production in other parts of the world that was stimulated by the inordinately high prices here.

But the heavy mortgage debt remained. The level of farm prices was remarkably steady from 1923 through 1929, as was the income from agriculture. But relatively little had been accomplished toward whittling down the outstanding farm debt. The large volume of "frozen" farm mortgages was an important contributing factor to the freezing of bank assets for, unfortunately and most unwisely, commercial banks had been permitted, by state and federal legislation of the 1920's, to buy and hold such mortgages as an asset against their demand liabilities.

We do not now debate the wisdom or propriety of the farm relief measures that were undertaken in the 1930's. The government was bailing out business concerns through the RFC, it was bailing out home owners through the HOLC, and these precedents warranted action to bail out the farmers. All of these bailing-out measures were part of a general program of "reflation," as it was called, whereby active inflationary steps were taken to restore economic health by large injections of new money into the economy.

If the matter had stopped there, less damage would have been done. The HOLC has long since been put in liquidation, and the RFC should have been. But the farm subsidy policy did not stop where it should have stopped. It became the vehicle for the application of various dangerous economic fallacies and mischievous concepts that have now become strongly entrenched politically, although their economic unsoundness and unwisdom are generally recognized by farmers, as individuals, and by some others.

It began with the pernicious doctrine that the way to increase farm income was to restore agricultural prosperity through scarcity. This involved the government in the worst of all economic conspiracies, that of the wanton destruction of goods to hold prices up. The first act of this sort was the plowing under of cotton and the slaughter of pigs, done at a time when political capital was being made of the third of the nation that was underfed and underclothed. From this amateurish beginning the policy of wanton waste has been raised to a professional status by the widespread destruction committed by the Commodity Credit Corporation, which has regularly allowed spoilage of immense quantities of butter, eggs, and other perishables, and has regularly destroyed, openly and without shame, millions of bushels of potatoes.

A seemingly sound foundation was laid for the agricultural subsidy program by the concept of parity. At first this was stated as parity of income—farmers should have the same income, in relation to a base period, as nonfarm economic groups had in relation to their income in that base period. This device was a statistical fraud. It was changed later to parity of purchasing power—the prices received by farmers should always be in a "parity" relationship to the prices paid by farmers for the goods they bought.

The principal result of this statistical contraption has been to set in motion a wage-price spiral that cannot be stopped as long as the fundamentally unsound premises go unchallenged. Every increase of wages adds to the prices paid by farmers, and thus leads to a higher parity price for farm products. This, in turn, creates a case for further wage increases. Government has become an active participant in, and promoter of, this criminal conspiracy against the consumers. Even without the excuse of a war, there would eventually have emerged a powerful demand for government control and regulation of both prices and wages.

The only proper solution is a return to the free market for the products of both the farm and the factory. This includes, also, a free market for labor. The only long-term basis of a prosperous agriculture is a free, prosperous economy. Government supports have already led to a dangerous degree of regimentation for the farmers. They cannot long remain free if government, for whatever ostensibly benevolent motives, acquires the power to dictate where and how much to sow and reap, where and for what price to sell, and to set these terms for the pottage of price or income support.

DIRECT GOVERNMENT PARTICIPATION IN BUSINESS

The third area in which there is no proper place for government is the direct use of the people's money to acquire and operate business enterprises in competition with taxpaying business. This direct advance into the socialist state has been made under various pretenses of benevolence, none of which can be justified except in the light of the socialist doctrine.

For example, much was said at one time to the effect that the prices and profits of private business were too high, hence government should establish "yardstick" enterprises to demonstrate how consumers would benefit from the greater efficiency of public ownership.

Another line of supporting argument has been that public business enterprise is proper when developed in connection with other activities such as flood control, improvement of navigation, and the national defense.

Finally, a third contention has been that where the economy needs more of a given commodity, e.g., steel or aluminum, and private investors will not provide the necessary expansion of productive facilities, the government should proceed to do so.

UNDER WHATEVER system of government the people live, there must be production. The socialist contention is that there will be greater production *in toto* with government ownership of all productive equipment and management of all productive operations than there will be if capital ownership and managerial direction are under private control. It is precisely this contention that underlies the yardstick doctrine, namely, that government operation is more efficient than private, and hence there should be government-owned plants in various fields to demonstrate what the savings to consumers would be if all production were under public ownership and management. Among the first ventures into the direct application of the socialist tenet were the government-owned power plants. There have also been suggestions that the government enter the steel and other industries.

It is an elementary economic fact that all production involves cost. Ordinarily, the consumers of the good or service will pay a price that enables the producer to recover the cost. But it is not necessary that the consumers pay the full cost, *provided* part of it is paid by someone else. In the case of government-owned plants that sell their product to consumers at attractive prices, the balance of the cost is carried by the federal taxpayers. Here is the deceitful "come on" of the government business ventures which purport to be demonstrations of the superior efficiency of public over private management.

The source of the deception is in government's disregard of various costs which must be met by private enterprise if it is to survive. There is disregard by government construction agencies of initial construction costs that has been demonstrated widely, from the cost per bed in veterans' hospitals to the cost per KWH of productive capacity in power plants.

Then there is dissipation of capital. Private management must conserve its capital because stockholders do not condone recklessness, nor do they willingly replace lost or wasted capital. Government simply draws on the taxpayers or restores the dissipated capital by increasing the public debt. Billions of dollars have thus been written off on behalf of the Reconstruction Finance Corporation, the Commodity Credit Corporation, and other federal agencies.

Another source of apparent government advantage is in the absence of any obligation to earn a return for those who have provided the capital. Private management must seek a profit out of which to reward those who have supplied the capital. This is a necessary condition for the maintenance of the investment flow. Private citizens base their decisions regarding investment upon the relative profit prospects. They thus channel capital formation into those lines which are of greatest general advantage. Government does not consult those who must supply its capital funds—the taxpayers—as to their preference or their readiness to make a particular application of them. It is often said that government acts from broader, more benevolent motives and hence secures a greater general advantage than would be obtained through the profit motive.

The real motive has not been primarily to increase the output of goods and services in the economy. Having no capital funds of its own, it is sheer arrogance for a political party in power to assume that it can siphon off private funds through taxation or borrowing and use them in a better job of production than private business management can do. The real purpose is not greater production or production at less actual cost, but the distribution of favors and benefits to particular sections or groups on terms, ostensibly but not actually, more advantageous than could be set by private enterprise.

Finally, government pays no taxes and in view of the immense tax load that private business and individuals must carry, a load made heavier by the added burden of the deficits in government business undertakings, it becomes evident that there can be no reasonable comparison of relative efficiency on the basis of prices charged by public and private industry, respectively. Every representation or pretense of such greater efficiency is a fraud against the people. A political party that consents to be a participant in such fraud is betraying its trust and has no rightful claim to public confidence.

The second case, that of government ownership and operation of all the facilities that might be developed as an incident of other major facilities such as flood control and improvement of navigation will not hold water. The inconsistency of objective between flood control and power production has often been pointed out. Yet planning and construction of multiple purpose projects continue. In fact, the great zeal for expanded power production has been a factor in the relative failure of the flood control program to accomplish its purpose. Even if there should be a good case, in certain situations, for the installation of generators and the production of electric energy, this still provides no warrant for federal entrance into the business of distribution and sale of such power. The Hoover Commission task force on Water Resources Projects recommended that the states should control all non-navigation uses of water at government reservoirs and that the power developed at government dams should be marketed through the facilities of private companies. These recommendations are thoroughly sound.

The third case, which is government production in the event of shortages which private investment is supposedly not able or willing to provide, is in the realm of fantasy. The shortage which some government agency may allege to exist would require careful examination by unbiased experts. The best test of this condition is the price of the commodity in a free market. If that price were to stand at an abnormally high level for a considerable time it would indicate a genuine shortage of production. But that condition would also be the kind of demonstration to which private investors would be most likely to respond by providing more productive capacity. Short-run scarcities and temporary price flurries would not justify additional large-scale investment by either private investors or the government. The former would be smart enough to know the difference.

REINTERPRET THE GENERAL WELFARE

The development of large-scale government lending and giving, and also the extravagant use of the people's money to engage in ruinous competition with them, has occurred over the past two decades. There had been grants and subsidies in earlier periods of the national history, but they represented only a negligible proportion of the total federal spending until the depression of the early 1930's provided the opportunity and, for the time, the excuse. Insofar as the depressed conditions of the 1930's afforded a warrant for federal grants and subsidies, the passing of these conditions should have been the signal for their termination. There has been no termination, but rather a continuous growth, entrenchment, and consolidation of these activities and their cost. This demoralizing trend must be stopped for it can lead, in the end, only to complete submergence of the individual by making him completely dependent on government. Dependence means loss of freedom just as independence means the full realization of freedom.

THE DEFENSE of the immense scale to which federal lending, giving, and competing with private business have attained has been that these activities have been in promotion of the general welfare. But all that government does is presumably in furtherance of this broad purpose. The funds that government spends for defense, the administration of justice, highways, and education are obtained from the people through taxes or loans. But it does not follow that anything whatever that government may choose to do with the people's money is a promotion of the general welfare just because certain uses of that money are.

A vital distinction is lost sight of when the general welfare is interpreted too broadly. It is the distinction between those services that are assigned to government because private persons or groups cannot do them efficiently, or should not be permitted to undertake them because too much power over others would be involved; and those other activities that can be competently performed privately without undue exercise of autocratic power. In the first group are such functions as defense, justice, coinage, weights and measures, and the regulation of interstate commerce. In the second group is the whole range of private business enterprise. There is no assured promotion of general welfare when government goes beyond its own proper functions to engage in activities that can be better done by private individuals or agencies.

Although the general welfare may be the ostensible objective, the actual result of these extensions of governmental activities is to promote the socialist goal of redistributing wealth and income. This result is evident when government takes one person's income and lends it to another at a low rate, or on terms that disregard security of repayment; or when it takes money from some and distributes it as grants or subsidies to others; or when it uses tax revenues to compete on ruinous terms with taxpayers.

Such practices do not promote the general welfare. They undermine it. The only sound basis for a wholesome, advancing general welfare is a steady increase of production that enlarges the supply of goods and services on which genuine welfare depends and that creates the income with which the people can meet their own needs without being dependent on the deceptive benevolence of government, or under its control as the recipients of its paternalistic bounty.

REDUCE FEDERAL PERSONNEL

Another important step along the road to less government is to reduce the number of public employees. This number has increased alarmingly, especially over the past two decades. Insofar as the growth has been a product of the expansion of both proper and improper federal services, the curtailment or elimination of these services should bring a corresponding reduction of personnel. Other causes of the increase are less obvious and hence more difficult to combat. Among these are: (1) the creation of multiple agencies to perform the same or similar services; (2) the practice of determining salary increases according to the number of employees supervised; (3) the advantage that a huge federal personnel and payroll give in the propaganda to retain big government and further increase it.

IT IS obviously wasteful to hire more people to do a job than are really needed to do the job well. Yet the federal government has a system which makes certain that more will be hired than are needed. This is the determination of the salaries of bureau chiefs, section heads, and other supervisory personnel by the number of employees under their direction. It is fantastic that this should be tolerated in the country that has learned more, and gained more, from efficiency management than any other country on earth. At the beginning there may have been some vague notion about a relationship between the number of workers and the quantity and quality of work done. If so, it was unsound at the outset and it is no longer regarded as applicable. This device makes certain that much of the energy of supervisory heads will go into the scheming and contriving whereby the number under their direction will be increased rather than into doing the best possible job at the lowest cost.

The growth of duplicate and multiple agencies doing essentially the same thing has been both a cause and a result of big government. As the scope and complexity of the federal organization increased, it was easier to create a new agency than to expend enough thought and energy on adaptation of the existing administrative organization to render the new agency unnecessary. As this process went on an adequate grasp of the entire federal structure became progressively difficult and the wasteful duplications multiplied unchecked.

The political advantage of a huge number of federal employees as the firm, continuing nucleus of a propaganda machine is evident. Granting the assumption that party managers are likely to make, namely, that these federal employees will vote solidly for the regime in power in order to be assured of their jobs, this assumption is not conclusive as to the real advantage. If more people are employed and paid than can be justified by the amount or importance of the work done, it follows that nothing useful is being created. Yet they have their pay as income to spend and they compete with bona fide workers and producers for a share of the product of the latter. The real producers must carry a double burden: first, the taxes to support the useless public employees; and second, the higher prices that everyone must pay because of those consumers whose income does not represent an addition to the supply of goods in the market.

REORGANIZE DEPARTMENTS AND AGENCIES

The various government departments and agencies should be reorganized internally to establish clear lines of authority and responsibility. Reorganization has been a favorite topic of reformers for half a century. Too frequently the term has served as a symbol of dissatisfaction rather than as a slogan of effective action. The current conception of "reorganization" goes little farther than shuffling and regrouping of agencies. It is seldom indeed that agencies are abolished, and it is futile to suppose that a badly organized, or an unnecessary, agency will be any better managed, or any more useful, if attached to one department rather than some other. The test of achievement by the party in power must include the way the departments and agencies are run as well as the record of bills rejected or passed by the Congress.

FROM THE standpoint of managerial operation, there is a reasonably apt parallel between government and business. In each case there is a co-ordination of various kinds of labor, and the use of more or less of material things, to the end that there shall be a certain output of goods or services. We pass over here the vast difference between private and public management with respect to motivation, although beyond doubt government would cost far less and command more respect among the citizens if public management were more fully imbued than it is with the concern for cost that permeates private management. The occasional, but fast-diminishing references to businesslike government are nostalgic reminiscences of a departed epoch when some thought that this ideal was a possibility.

The particular point to be stressed here is that the several federal departments and agencies, many of which are larger in point of funds handled annually than most of our private business enterprises, should be reorganized internally to establish clear lines of authority and responsibility. The Hoover Commission emphasized the defects that have developed in its report on *General Management of the Executive Branch*, submitted to the Congress in February, 1949. The fact that this Commission was deemed necessary, and the further fact that many separate surveys of departments and agencies have been made in recent years by private firms specializing in efficiency management, together constitute a serious indictment of our theory and practice of government. This indictment runs against the party in power. The whole emphasis of this book is that the party in power at any given time *is* the government in action.

Our great weakness has been that party control of the government has been regarded as a "plunderbund," a free and joyous ride for the faithful, and not as the assumption of a great responsibility to do the things that government should do for the people at the lowest possible cost to them. Little wonder that the duplicating and overlapping agencies have spawned so freely, that the Congress has met each new situation by creating another administrative unit, that a chaotic condition has developed which no one can reduce to order and system.

The party in power has created this chaos and is responsible for it. Any other party, aspiring to be the government in action, cannot evade or escape the responsibility of a thorough house cleaning within each department and also with respect to the scandalous duplications and multiplications of overlapping agencies.

Section 2

THE ROAD TO BETTER GOVERNMENT

HAVING POSTULATED that the area of federal government services and activities must be reduced, as the only way to better and less costly government, it becomes necessary to be somewhat specific as to what the functions and services of the federal government should be. This is a large subject but there is no more important matter, for upon it hinges the whole issue of the liberation of the individual from the encroachments of government, and the reversal of the trend that is now sweeping on so relentlessly to the undesired but seemingly inevitable goal of the socialist state.

BETTER GOVERNMENT THROUGH LESS GOVERNMENT

The major premise of this program is that the salvation of the individual as a free person lies in reducing the scope, the burden, and the absolutism of governmental powers over him. There must be less government. This means that the area of the things that government undertakes to do must be restricted to very much less than its present dimensions. At the same time, there must be a higher standard of performance of the services that are to be rendered by government. These matters are closely connected. Government costs too much because it is too big to be competently managed. Improved standards of operation are impossible unless the scope of government is reduced to manageable proportions.

THE FIRST STEP on the road to better government is to ensure that there is less government. This means a restriction of the scope of government action, a reduction of the things that government does, or tries to do. The poor job that government is doing—and let no one be deceived, it is a poor job—is because of the immense range and area over which the government effort is expended. There is no human capacity equal to the task of managing and supervising all of this effort so as to make it efficient and truly productive. Unless and until government has been whittled down to dimensions that can be comprehended, brought under effective control, and properly supervised, there is no way by which its sprawling growth can be halted. It will continually become more inefficient, more costly, more autocratic from the sheer weight of its directives and controls.

The growth of the inchoate federal organization has been, in large measure, unplanned. It has been easier to create another agency than to find the way, through careful study, to get certain things done as well or better by some existing agency. This has been true, also, of appropriations. It has been easier to pass another appropriation, or establish another fund, than to do the spade work needed to discover how the job could be better done under an existing appropriation. These lines of least resistance have offered seeming collateral advantages because the lazy way has created more federal jobs, it has fitted perfectly into the bureaucratic devices for promotion in rank and salary by increasing the number of employees to be supervised, and it has made more business for the contractors and suppliers whose chief contacts have been with federal procurement.

Undeniably, there has been a substantial degree of popular acceptance of this abnormal, unwholesome, and unduly costly expansion of the federal government. This acceptance can be attributed to various causes: (1) a decline of individual and community responsibility that has led to a surrender into the federal sphere of services that should have been kept at home; (2) a vicious spiral of heavier federal taxes and progressive depletion of state and local revenue potential that has made the states and localities more dependent on federal aid and also more willing to let Uncle Sam do it; (3) a temporary deterioration of the national character expressed through a marked preference for security regardless of the price paid for it.

One of the major tasks confronting the party that would reduce the federal government to proper and manageable size by eliminating useless, or overlapping, or unduly costly agencies and activities is that of combatting and overthrowing the current popular attitude. It is far from impossible to do this, although it will be difficult because of the readiness that virtually all political leaders in both parties have shown in promoting the false doctrine that the government can and should carry the people's burdens.

THE STATES MUST BE PRESERVED

In arriving at conclusions with respect to the proper scope of the federal functions, services, and powers, we should never forget, nor allow others to forget, the historic character of our federal system. The central government was created by a union of the states. All citizens should know at least these essential historical facts: (1) that this union almost did not happen; (2) that our great progress as a nation has come because it did happen; (3) that the states are still the sovereign units that comprise the nation which we know as the United States.

In order that there shall always be an "indivisible and indestructible union," in Daniel Webster's phrase, the states must be protected against an extreme absorption of power, resources, and control by the federal government.

THE STEADY and rapid aggrandizement of federal power has gone on, especially during the past generation, with little or no regard for the rights, or the duties and capabilities, of the states. The record of this expansion may be traced in the taxes collected by the federal government, and by the states and their local units, respectively. This record for selected years since 1890 is as follows:

Total Volume of Taxation in the United States
(Millions)

Taxing Authority	Years						
	1890	1913	1922	1926	1932	1940	1950
Federal	$374	$ 668	$3,487	$3,207	$1,809	$ 4,922	$35,091
State	96	307	858	1,264	1,890	3,313	7,939
Local	405	1,219	3,157	4,084	4,468	4,494	8,100
Total	$875	$2,194	$7,502	$8,555	$8,167	$12,729	$51,130

Sources: Years 1890 through 1926, National Industrial Conference Board, *The Cost of Government in the United States,* New York, 1927; later years, Bureau of the Census and Treasury Department.

The war years are intentionally omitted from this comparison. The record shows that during the periods of peace, the center of fiscal gravity was in the state and local governments until the 1930's of the present century. Today the federal government is collecting about three-fourths of all taxes levied on the people. The center of fiscal gravity has shifted from Main Street to Washington. Accompanying this change in the control over fiscal resources has been a continuous impairment of the ability of the states and their local subdivisions to support themselves and perform their own services out of tax resources available to them.

Federal expansion has been, in part, a product of two World Wars and of necessary steps to assure the future national security. But it has also been, in part, a product of the itch for power. The costs of past wars and of the current program of national defense belong in the federal budget. Aside from the questions properly to be asked regarding the prudence displayed in the use of our resources for these purposes, there can be no issue of their need or propriety. The real danger does not lie so much in these expenditures as in the nonmilitary spending which has been the means of usurping into federal control, services and resources that should remain with the states.

The technique of socialization requires as a first step that the resistance of local units be broken. Impairment of local fiscal resources is a frontal attack on local independence. There is no risk whatever that any of the states would ever transform itself into a socialist commonwealth. It will be done at the national level if it ever comes, and the continued concentration of fiscal resources and administrative powers in the federal government is an essential first step toward complete socialization. The socialists have understood this and they have abetted it. Others who have had a part in the process are not socialists and they have been ignorant of the consequences. The outcome will be the same, however, whether the steps toward it have been taken in ignorance or with design.

THE ESSENTIALS OF GOVERNMENT

The naked essentials of government are the administration of justice, the preservation of order, the national defense, and the collection of the taxes required to support these basic governmental services.

IN THIS preliminary approach to a definition of the proper fields of federal government action, a certain historical perspective is desirable. To this end let us consider first an eighteenth century conception of the functions of government, as expressed in the title of a series of lectures by Adam Smith, written about 1766. This title was: "Justice, Police, Revenue, and Arms."

The reason these primary governmental functions are so basic is that they are the rock bottom functions or services which the people must have, but which cannot be left to private action to provide. With respect to justice and internal order, it was all summed up long ago in the saying: "No man may take the law into his own hands." No man may seek what he regards as justice at point of knife or pistol. From the first stages of organized society, even in such primitive form as a mining camp, it was soon perceived that there could be neither justice nor internal order without organization. But the vigilantes shortly gave way to the sheriff. Informal organization was always succeeded by a more formal organization under duly constituted authority.

It is equally obvious that external security cannot be left to individual or group action. The national defense and security involve collective action and in modern times this has required complete national mobilization, for it has been increasingly true, unfortunately, that there are no noncombatants in total war. There must be a central organizing and directing head of the whole of the national resources of materials, manpower, and productive resources in the event of war.

The great problem, so far as concerns the centralized control of national resources for war, is to prevent a degree of militarization in advance of, or in preparation for war that would transform the nation into a "garrison state." Risk is an unavoidable aspect of freedom and the risk of being plunged into war is one that must be taken in determining the distribution of productive resources, during peacetime, between military and civilian requirements. A good rule for making this distribution is—at all times enough, but never too much, for the military.

NATIONAL DEFENSE AND SECURITY

The paramount service or function that only the federal government can perform is to provide for the national defense and security. The Constitution recognizes the right of each state to establish and maintain its own militia. Among the inherent powers of sovereignty is the police power under which, in every state, suitable state and local agencies have been created to safeguard the public safety, the public health, and public morals. These recognized state and local powers are mainly designed to promote internal or domestic security. They supplement, but they can never be a substitute for, the broad powers which the nation as a unit must possess and exercise for the defense and security of all. The most important practical issue in the area of national defense is the preservation of a proper balance between civilian control and military efficiency.

THE CONSTITUTION contains, in various places, recognition of an intent to establish the supremacy of the civilian officers of govment over the military establishment. The President, a civilian official, is commander-in-chief of all armed forces. The authority to declare war is vested in the Congress. This right is less significant today than it was when the formalities of ultimatum and an official declaration of war were generally observed preliminaries to armed conflict. The Constitution also limits appropriations for military purposes to two years.

It is highly important that the historic policy of civilian control be always maintained. But this raises a further question, namely, how far, and to what matters, shall the civilian control extend? There are two aspects of this question.

The first is that since military action is an implementation of foreign policy, at what point, if ever, does military advantage become paramount to the policy? Merely to state this question is to emphasize the importance of a logical, consistent foreign policy which, if clearly described and firmly pursued, may (1) prevent war, or (2) assure the most vigorous and successful prosecution of war if it should be unavoidable.

The second aspect of the issue indicated above regarding the degree of civilian control over the military establishment involves the proportion of the national resources to be allotted to military purposes. This is, in short, the financial or cost factor. War is essentially destructive. The objective of military operations is to achieve victory even if it should involve maximum destruction. The control of military costs that is most constructive and important is that which distinguishes between the necessary expendibility of materiel in action and the unnecessary, wasteful procurement and use of resources when no clear emergency is confronted. The records of military purchasing and of surplus military stocks are conclusive evidence of the improvidence of unrestrained purchasing. Inasmuch as this kind of control is indubitably a function and responsibility of the higher civilian authority, failure to exercise it is a plain dereliction of duty.

A FREE ECONOMY IS THE STRONGEST ECONOMY

The national defense and security involve more than military preparation. They involve also the preservation of a free economy. If the people are to lose their freedom, the devotion of resources to military effort will have been in vain. The loss of freedom may come as a result of defeat in war, or it may come from the imposition of severe controls and drastic regimentation. In the one case the condition of a "garrison state" will have been imposed by victorious conquerors. In the other it will have been imposed by the people's own military and political leaders.

A NATION's military establishment, though indispensable, is only its first line of defense. Its capacity to produce is the basic protection against attack and the ultimate arbiter of its destiny in the test of arms.

Primarily, production requires capital plant and equipment, developed resources, and the skills of labor and management.

But these primary factors are available in both the slave and the free nations. More is needed, however, than the technical apparatus and skills of production. This extra, essential ingredient of productive capacity is the freedom of a free economy. It is this that enables a nation of free men always to outproduce a nation of regimented, unfree men.

There is great temptation, in times of crisis, to abrogate freedom on the ground that a greater total effort will thus be achieved. This is both illusory and dangerous. The illusion comes from the belief that government can manage the economy better than free citizens can, hence the innumerable controls, restrictions, and regulations that impede more than they further production. The danger comes from the breach that is made in the fabric of freedom. Dictators and planners have long known that seduction of a free people to forego their freedom must be subtle and insidious. Fears must be played upon; a succession of emergencies and crises must be paraded, with resort to fiction where fact fails; prejudice must be amply supplied with material on which to grow. By taking away only a part at a time the gradual encroachment may be tolerated.

Central power and control grow by not giving back as much as was taken. Rent control was not abandoned after World War II. The Congress enacted, after Korea, more sweeping controls over the economy than those of the second World War, although the situation was still far short of all-out war. How many, and which ones, will be retained this time after the war threat is ended?

Power corrupts and absolute power corrupts absolutely. Even in time of crisis the people must steadily resist the surrender of their basic freedoms, for in yielding they are undermining the true source of national strength and superiority. Support of this resistance must be a cardinal policy of a party that would stand for the individual against the state.

PAYING AS WE GO

Next to the hard lesson of the futility and danger of resort to controls in a critical or emergency situation is the equally hard lesson that there is no easy way to meet the cost of coping with such a situation. Many believe that this cost can be lightened if it can be postponed, which obviously means using loans rather than taxes. The error in this belief is compounded when there is added the contention that future generations, being beneficiaries of the policies that involve the cost, should contribute to it. The central issue here again is that of keeping or losing the freedoms of a free economy. Bankruptcy is an enemy of freedom. Paying as we go for defense, or war, or any other national emergency, is the only safe way to avoid bankruptcy, and hence the only sure way to protect our freedoms.

THE IDEA that borrowing to finance the cost of defense, war, or other national emergency is less burdensome than taxing owes its appeal to wishful thinking rather than to factual analysis. Actually, loan financing does not postpone the real burden. Moreover, it makes the burden heavier.

The real burden which enlarged government operations lay on the people is the deprivation caused by greater government use of goods and services. Both government and the people must at all times be supported out of current production. When the government demand is greatly expanded, as in an enlarged military program, less is available out of current product for civilian use. This is the real burden. It must be borne now. There is no more chance of postponing it than there is of equipping soldiers today with guns, tanks, and planes out of next year's steel production.

By the same logic, the levy of taxes to pay for what government takes is only the financial parallel of the diversion of goods and services. To whatever extent these commodities are not available for civilian use, the failure to siphon off private income correspondingly through taxes would leave income in private hands that could be used only to bid up prices. Since the deficiency in taxation would indicate that government had borrowed the funds to pay for part of its total acquisition there would be, by so much, an addition to the purchasing power in private hands. And if the loan funds were obtained from the commercial banks the foundation of a further inflation would be laid. In fact, government loans purchased out of private savings definitely not put aside for consumption use by their owners are likewise inflationary, since government expenditure of these funds releases them into the consumption stream.

The wishful thinkers turn at this point to controls. They should know from experience here and elsewhere that no system of controls has ever prevented black markets, which are the rampant expression of inflation. It is possible to prevent inflation but not to control it. Paying as we go will prevent inflation by making loans unnecessary.

The burden of loan financing is heavier than the tax burden, first, because inflation is always a heavier, more inequitably distributed burden than taxation, and second, because it saddles the future with an enormous budgetary charge for interest on a debt that cannot be repaid.

Inflation is inevitable with large-scale loan financing. It destroys savings, the purchasing power of pensions, social security benefits, and insurance. It impoverishes millions and their despair is a fertile seed ground for the lying "isms" that seek the destruction of our freedoms.

FOREIGN POLICY

A nation's foreign policy is the core of its defense problem. This policy is, at the same time, the most difficult of all matters of government because it can never be a wholly unilateral determination. The national aims and aspirations of other countries are always present as complicating, and at times overruling considerations. The fact that foreign policy must ever be designed and exhibited in the international arena where widely diverse national interests, economic and political, are encountered makes it supremely important that this policy be intelligible to all, consistent within itself as a whole, and unmistakably clear as to our own purposes and objectives. There must be no vacillation, neither weakness nor truculence, and above all, no double-dealing.

THE STATEMENT that a nation's foreign policy is the core of its defense problem means that this policy is usually an influential, and sometimes a determining, factor as to whether or not there will be war. Through its foreign policy a nation discovers both its allies and its potential enemies. International conflicts are, in modern times, struggles between the "have" and the "have-not" nations. The aggressors responsible for starting World Wars I and II were "have-nots." They had ample evidence of weakness and indecision in the foreign policies of the "have" nations and they gambled on these defects. In each case they almost won. In neither case would they have dared the issue of war if the United States alone, leaving all other nations aside, had had a clear concept of what global war means and a firm determination that such a catastrophe must not be allowed to happen.

We cannot now rewrite history, but only hope that we may profit from knowing the record. What we must do, and all that we can do now, is to write off these bitterly costly mistakes and resolve that no more such shall be made. We know now that no one wins in war, not even those who write the terms of armistice or surrender. This nation will always be poorer and weaker for lack of the unbegotten sons of the young men who died in the Argonne, on the Normandy beaches, and in Korea.

The elements of sound foreign policy for the United States are these:

1. This nation does not seek war. Its hope is for peace. However, it will not avoid war at the price of appeasement.

2. This nation seeks no more territory. Our release of Cuba and the Philippines is lasting evidence that we want no colonies.

3. This nation will not engage in aggression, neither will it remain passive when aggressive moves are made by others, for such moves always carry the threat of another global war.

4. This nation will join in any open, honest commitment to reduce and limit armaments and to end the senseless competition in military construction.

5. This nation supports the United Nations as an agency for the promotion of peace and for the adjustment of claims, differences and all sources of friction which, unless settled by peaceful means, may lead to war.

Section 3

THE ROAD TO PROPER FEDERAL
FUNCTIONS

THE PRESENT section is the final installment of the platform or
program designed to protect the individual from overwhelming
encroachment by the state. Reduction of the size, power, and
cost of the central government must be accomplished to make
this protection secure. In addition, some further applications
are required of the test proposed above for determining the
propriety of federal performance of given services or functions.
In the present section these applications are made with respect
to each of three major fields, namely, the promotion of business
and economic activities, the conservation of natural resources,
and social welfare.

In each of these fields the main task is to determine just how
the federal government should operate. In general, its role
should be that of regulation and supervision and not participation. Even here, however, the keynote must be patience and restraint, lest an excess of regulatory detail, in combination with
the crushing tax load, should so effectively dampen the enterprise spirit as to provide a spurious case for government participation in business activities.

The characteristic lines of federal activity should include:

1. Stimulus and leadership.
2. Pilot demonstrations, such as mine safety, forest management, and highway construction standards.

3. The enforcement of laws supporting the legitimate federal functions.

4. The supreme judicial function—interpretation of the Constitution and review of lower court decisions that involve constitutional issues.

TESTS OF PROPER FEDERAL FUNCTIONS

The internal or domestic functions of the federal government properly include those matters pertaining to the maintenance of a stable and orderly society which transcend the legal jurisdictions of the several states. The distinction between the functions which should be assigned to the federal government and those which may be left to the states is not always sharp and clear. Virtually all of the domestic functions, now within the federal sphere— whether by constitutional provision, judicial construction, or assumption by common consent—could in fact be performed by the various states. The most important test by which to determine whether a given function should be in the federal or the state sphere is the effect on the rights and interests of the citizens of the several states.

THE MOST serious domestic problem confronting the people of the United States is that of defining the proper area of federal functions. Yet this problem must be promptly and correctly dealt with if the destructive trend toward an all-powerful federalism is to be halted and reversed.

The basic, underlying objective is the preservation of a free economy and a free society. The test suggested here to determine the proper federal functions, namely, the effect on the rights and interests of the citizens of the several states, is designed to further attainment of this objective.

For example, it would be possible for each state to have its own coinage, its own system of weights and measures, its own bankruptcy code, and its own postal system. If this were the situation, however, the rights and interests of all citizens would be adversely affected. The market area would be greatly restricted, the flow of capital investment would be seriously impeded, personal and business communications would be hampered, and even travel among the states for personal or business reasons would involve much inconvenience.

Federal regulation of bona fide interstate commerce is proper and necessary because thereby the rights and interests of all citizens are protected. Unfortunately, judicial construction of this power has gone beyond any reasonable and proper definition and has become the basis of unwarranted federal control over purely local business transactions.

The existence of a problem or a need common to all of the people is not ground, however, for federal performance or intervention. Murder, arson, burglary, embezzlement, and other offenses against persons and property are violations of the good social order. They can be and are adequately dealt with under state law. They provide no case for federal participation or control.

Likewise, education, public health, dependency relief, and fire protection are common needs. None of them, however, is a proper subject of federal performance and control. State and local authority is entirely competent to handle them.

These illustrations serve to elucidate the test proposed here. The essential point is that federal authority and control become necessary and logical where relegation of authority to the states would produce conditions clearly adverse to the rights and interests of the citizens in ways that would negate the basic national objective of a free economy and a free society.

POLICING ECONOMIC AND BUSINESS ACTIVITIES

Economic and business activity normally requires no stimulative action by government. The driving power of the private economic incentives is enormous, particularly under the spur of the acquisitive proclivities of individuals. The principal problems that should have the attention and concern of government are:

1. To keep open the channels through which this driving power may freely operate.

2. To curb improper or irresponsible deviations without blocking the main channel.

These problems involve a grave responsibility for government. Their solution requires an acceptance of the nature and propriety of business profit that is likely to run counter to the prejudice and misinformation of politicians and of some citizens, who would much prefer to believe that government can curb profits through taxation or regulation without depriving the people of the material goods that are produced by private enterprise.

THERE IS A rightful place and responsibility of government in the field of economic and business activity, but it is not often properly understood and evaluated. This rightful place is to keep the privately generated forces within the proper channel. It is, essentially, a policing function.

The Constitution provides for federal regulation of interstate commerce, a uniform system of weights and measures, a uniform currency, and a uniform code of bankruptcy procedure. But the words "monopoly" and "trust" do not occur in the Constitution. This instrument would be read in vain for such terms as "securities and exchange," "fair trade practices," "parity prices," "unfair labor practices," "small business," "progressive taxation," and scores of other terms and concepts found in the reams of legislation enacted annually.

The recital of these few illustrative terms is sufficient to indicate the extent to which the federal government has gone beyond its proper constitutional purposes and obligations in the area of economic and business activities. In virtually every case we have a situation in which there has been a popular demand —either spontaneous or inspired—for the seemingly easy way of more government control and regulation instead of the slower, but eventually more effective method of private competitive action. What the people have not recognized in their impatience for quick relief and their naïve, misplaced faith in the beneficence of government, is that they have been surrendering segments of their birthright of freedom for a series of messes of pottage.

Two instances must suffice. The first is monopoly. In the long history of this concept it has become identified with capital, because for centuries capital was the scarce productive factor and its owners were able to dictate their own terms. The Antitrust Act of 1890—the Sherman Act—is the basis of present federal legislation. This Act makes conspiracies in restraint of trade unlawful. It has always been construed and applied by the Department of Justice as relating only to conspiracies of capitalists. The Supreme Court has obligingly held that labor organizations cannot be guilty of conspiracy under this legislation, although there are no more obvious conspiracies in restraint of trade than the nation-wide strikes that any of a dozen labor bosses may order at will.

A second illustration is the assumption of wholly unwarranted powers by the Federal Communications Commission in the field of radio and television. We are not here concerned with the relative merits of different technical devices, but solely with the impudent arrogance of federal bureaucrats. It has often been pointed out that if there had been a federal authority, fifty years ago, with comparable powers over the automobile industry and possessed of the dictatorial itch to forbid distribution of any automobile until it could be proved that the purchasers of this model would not be the losers because of mechanical or other shortcomings not detected and corrected by the manufacturer, the vast development of the motor vehicle that we have witnessed would not have occurred.

A measure of how far we have traveled along the road of government paternalism toward the goal of impotent, unproductive, sterile statism may be found in the contrast between the freedom of the older industries to grow by trial and error (with some of the errors discovered and reported by the thousands of customers who were using the early models), and the restrictions imposed by bungling bureaucracy upon the newer industries such as radio and television.

COMPETITION AND MONOPOLY

A healthy competition is essential to the efficient functioning of a free economy. Where this condition prevails, the rewards of effort in any business are determined primarily by the ability and the resources of the respective competitors. In a competitive system, also, profit performs its important function of guiding the flow of investment into the areas of production in which additional output will be most beneficial to consumers and most rewarding to both labor and capital.

The opposite or converse of competition is monopoly. Federal authority to deal with certain forms of monopoly has been based on the constitutional grant of power to the federal government to regulate commerce among the several states and with foreign nations. Some forms of monopoly are good, other forms are bad. The central issue is that of distinguishing between the beneficial and the injurious forms of monopoly and of dealing with the latter in such a way as to assure the fullest freedom of competition.

THE ESSENTIAL distinction between beneficial and injurious monopoly is established by applying the test of competition as the alternative. Wherever competition will result in a demonstrably greater over-all advantage to the people as workers and consumers, monopoly is obviously injurious.

It has been discovered through experience, however, that there are various fields of economic activity in which competition, if enforced, would be adverse to the best interests of consumers. These fields are described, collectively, as the "public utilities." It is far more economical, in terms of capital investment and in terms of cost and convenience to consumers, to have the supply of gas, water, electricity, or telephone service in a given area under a single management than to have several companies competing with each other in these various service operations in that area. And where there is the greatest efficiency of operation, it will be possible to pay the maximum wages.

The principle of monopoly in the utility industries has been fully recognized and thoroughly established. A co-ordinate principle, also thoroughly established, is that such monopolies should be regulated as to such matters as capital investment, rates or prices of services, and profit return. The regulatory responsibility is divided between federal and state authority by reference to the interstate concept.

Another form of tolerated monopoly is the system of patents, jurisdiction over which is delegated to the federal government by the Constitution. The theory underlying the patent, namely, that through the protection afforded thereby research, discovery, and invention are stimulated, is sound. But this protection is not in perpetuity. Eventually, any given patent expires.

In actual operation, however, many important patents are made available to competitors long before their expiration dates. The practice of licensing, and cross-licensing, of patents is found in many industries. Where this practice prevails, profit is not attributable to the ownership of patents, as such, but to the skill and aggressiveness of the competitive application of all the resources of capital and technology.

The basic test of monopoly that is adverse to the public interest is that set out in the Act of 1890—a contract, combination, or conspiracy in restraint of trade. Federal policy in the application of this test has been far from uniform and consistent. Sheer size has been construed, more than once, as prima facie evidence of an intent to restrain trade, regardless of the degree of competition actually existing. Prosecutions have been brought in some cases for reasons that were obviously political. In other cases prosecution has been permited to degenerate into persecution.

The current conception of concerted action to restrain trade still adheres to the traditional historical view that such action of an unlawful character is possible only by agreement among the owners and managers of capital. In this view the only possible monopoly is that acquired and exercised by capital.

Such was the case prior to the growth of labor organizations to a position of dominance over large masses of workers, and with great indirect influence over other groups of workers, exercised through such methods as the boycott, the sympathetic strike, and the industry-wide strike. Through these and other devices it is possible to bring about a concerted action by large numbers of workers that is as plainly a restraint of trade as would be any parallel move by a small group of industry managers or owners.

There can be no adequate development of a wholesome antimonopoly policy until it is recognized that sufficient power to throttle competition now vests in those who control labor as well as in those who control capital. The federal Antitrust Act must be administered without malice or favor. It must be directed against all cases of interference with the full and free play of interstate competition, whether the interference come from a combination or conspiracy of capital, or of labor.

FAIR PRICE AND TRADE PRACTICES

A corollary of the antimonopoly legislation has been the series of laws aimed at the preservation of competition by the policing of prices and other business practices. The services of an administrative agency are useful and necessary in the performance of this function, which is not an appropriate one to be vested in the Department of Justice. This Department should operate primarily as the prosecuting attorney for the government, and as its legal counselor. Essentially administrative activities lie outside its proper jurisdiction.

A high order of statemanship and of administrative probity is required for the kind of supervision and inspection that is involved in this patrol of the private economy. If these qualities exist, the task can be done though it would still involve serious difficulties. If they are absent, the operation is certain to sink to the low level of political and ideological bias. Such a decline has occurred. It must be corrected and reversed.

THE ULTIMATE objective of administrative inspection and supervision of prices and business practices generally, as an adjunct of enforcement of the antimonopoly statutes, is the discovery of actions that are likely, if unchecked, to lead to combination or conspiracy in restraint of trade. By and large, this kind of policing operation should be initiated upon complaint. There is sufficient freedom of speech in this country to assure that dealers or consumers, or both, will become aware of and report upon practices that deny to them the full advantage of competition. The duly constituted authority, in this case the Federal Trade Commission, goes beyond the proper limits of its jurisdiction when it mistakes size for monopoly, or when it confuses similarity of prices quoted by evenly matched competitors, for collusion to restrain trade. If the laws under which the Commission operates authorize such proceedings, then the laws are too broad.

Among the many forms taken by the quest for security, none is more illusory than the legislation intended to enforce fair prices and fair trade practices. The peoples of England and Western Europe went through all this centuries ago, when there was more drastic regulation of prices and trade practices than any we have yet devised. The result of the mediaeval enforcement of the "just price" was a static economy which lasted until the new wine of the Industrial Revolution burst the old bottle of mercantilistic regimentation.

Businessmen have been primarily responsible for this return to mediaevalism, since it is unlikely that the politicians would have had the temerity to initiate fair price and fair trade legislation except at the urgent insistence of some business interests.

It requires no great economic insight to perceive that all such legislation is a throttling of competition. It is true that competition takes many forms—advertising, attractiveness of displays, quality of wares, personality and aggressiveness of the sales force, and so on. But the chief competitive weapon is price. All of the other devices are subsidiary and relatively ineffective alone. When there is a legal requirement that all must sell a given article at the same price—whether this price is dictated by the manufacturer or by a public authority matters not—there is a denial of the essence of competition. There is a reversion to the static rigidity of the mediaeval controlled economy.

It is highly important that all legislative enforcement of prices be abandoned. Individual producers may then seek, if they wish, to enforce prices for their products. Without legislative support of such policies they are not likely to be widely successful. It is also of the utmost importance that the operations and activities of the Federal Trade Commission be confined to those genuinely related to the enforcement of the antimonopoly laws rather than be allowed to degenerate into a politically and ideologically inspired campaign of business control and persecution.

INFORMATIONAL SERVICES

An important service that the federal government can perform for the people is the collection and distribution of comprehensive, authoritative data relating to general business and to other conditions within the economy. Aside from routine reports of departments, the Census Bureau was for a long time the principal source of statistical and other data pertaining not only to the population but to other aspects of the nation's growth and development. Today, a legion of other agencies floods the country with statistics and all manner of other reading matter. This great expansion of publicity and publications has been a concomitant of the general advance of big government. And as it occurred the essential purpose of the federal fact-finding service has been lost. The grain of sound, useful material is buried in the chaff and straw of publications that are either trivial or definitely propagandist in character.

RELIABLE information is a useful and necessary aid to sound business decisions. The federal government has both the facilities and the responsibility to compile and distribute such information. This service, competently and objectively done, is beneficial to all. While methods of compilation, sampling, and estimating are never infallible, an "official government report" has long been recognized as the most authoritative source that could be given.

This standing must be jealously preserved. When government is concerned, as it always should be, with those matters that involve the genuine well-being of the people, there would be little reason to doubt its objectivity. But when it has become a colossus and when the further extension of its own power has become the major goal of its huge bureaucracy, there is no longer that scrupulous regard for relevance and pertinence which should characterize all that government does.

Because we have permitted the federal government to attain the colossal stage, a double-barreled deterioration of the federal informational services has occurred.

First, as a proliferation of trivia. The many departments and agencies have used, in the aggregate, large sums to finance the writing, publication, and distribution of booklets, pamphlets, and monographs on literally thousands of subjects and projects of such limited importance as to fail utterly to justify the cost.

Second, as a use of publicity techniques to further the aggrandizement of the federal government. The military departments have more than 3,000 persons, including civilian and uniformed personnel, engaged in publicity, advertising, and so-called public relations work. The total bill for these types of promotion by all government agencies is more than $100 million annually. The propagandist character of the material issued may be illustrated by the campaign of the Federal Security Administration for compulsory health insurance, that of the military department for universal military training, that of the Department of Agriculture for control of farm operations, and that of the Department of the Interior for greater federal ownership of electric power facilities.

The government's press agents are not subject to the limitations imposed upon private groups that may seek to influence legislation. The government agents are continually seeking to influence legislation, and always in the direction of a greater concentration of power, control, and resources in Washington.

The federal propaganda mill should be closed down. Federal statistical and reporting services should be restricted to objective fact-finding. There are at present too many of even this type of agency and a proper condensation and co-ordination would result in better informational service at less cost.

THE CONSERVATION OF NATURAL RESOURCES

The American people have become increasingly conservation-minded over the last fifty years. As this change of attitude occurred, the expenditures of government for conservation purposes steadily increased. A concomitant development was an enlargement of federal control, which usually had at the outset a bona fide conservation objective but which in many cases was eventually directed at other objectives under the cloak of conservation. The problem of government's sphere in the conservation of natural resources is this: How far can government go in the imposition of controls and restrictions upon private owners of property, under a program of resource conservation, and still preserve the essential freedoms of economic discretion and economic action that are necessary in a free, competitive-enterprise society?

BY THE END of the nineteenth century most of the land that was valuable for agriculture, forestry, or mining had passed into private ownership. Under an earlier conception of inexhaustibility, there had been waste and predatory exploitation. The active concern and vigorous leadership of private citizens and public officials were responsible for effecting a change of viewpoint and for inaugurating various conservation measures. With respect to bona fide conservation purposes, both federal and state governments have engaged in a variety of activities, over a wide front, which illustrate very well the proper function of government in this field. There has been extensive research in conservation techniques. The agricultural experiment stations, the Forest Service, and the Bureau of Mines are illustrative of this broad advance. In over-all, we have a good example of leadership, advice, and demonstration—the kind of service that it is appropriate for government to undertake in other fields as well as in conservation.

But the activities and expenditures of the federal government have been extended increasingly beyond the limits and purposes of bona fide conservation, although still largely under the guise of this objective. For example, in the case of agriculture, a substantial control has been built up through the regulations governing soil conservation payments, while at the same time the large expenditures made to protect the relative income status of individual farmers have contributed to more rapid exhaustion of basic soil resources by encouraging extreme cropping. In the case of water resources, a substantial portion of the expenditure has gone into facilities for government production and distribution of electric power in competition with private taxpaying business. As a result of this expansion in various directions, the federal government has become committed to the payment of large subsidies which, too often, have only a remote connection with conservation.

Subsidies involve controls and those who accept subsidies forego, to some extent, the rights and prerogatives of property ownership. Thus a proper and reasonable public service is distorted into an implement for shaping the all-powerful central state.

PUBLIC EDUCATION

The expression "social welfare" is inherently broad and in general usage it has been artificially extended. The essential content can be indicated, however, by the three fields of education, health, and dependency.

Education at public expense has long been an accepted policy in the United States. It is one of the governmental services that has, thus far, been retained at the state and local level. A good job has been done there and will continue to be done there if adequate state and local resources are provided.

The federal tax squeeze has led to demands for federal grants in aid of education. Even in the first bills to provide this aid, there were evidences of federal control. Once committed to a grant program, resistance to the further controls that would be inevitable would be difficult; and as the grants increased to a level at which dependence upon them would be complete, any degree of control that the federal bureaucracy might devise would have to be accepted.

The solution is to be found in a release of tax resources to the states and their local units, not in a federal grant in aid of local education costs.

HISTORICALLY, the service of education has been performed by private schools and colleges and by governmental units. Responsibility for education at public expense has been predominantly local, with provision by the states for training beyond the high school level. The cost of public education has been shared by local and state governments according to a variety of formulas. Complete control of curricula, school administration, and general educational policy has always been in the hands of local and state officials.

The argument made by proponents of a federal education grant to the states is that some states need financial assistance in order to maintain certain minimum education standards. It is entirely overlooked that a major reason for the inability of some states, or all states, to finance their own services is the fact that the federal taxes are already so heavy, particularly on incomes, as to restrict both the scope and the productivity of state and local taxes. Although a federal grant to aid the states with their education costs might begin as a moderate sum (the amount in bills heretofore introduced has been $300 million) it would eventually be many times that amount. The further increase of federal taxes required to pay the grant would complete the vicious circle. Instead of moving farther down the broad avenue of state dependency upon federal bounty, this trend should be reversed. Since the major part of the cost of public education falls upon the cities, the best way of enlarging the fiscal resources of cities to meet this burden would be federal withdrawal from the field of admissions and related taxes, leaving them to local use. They are admirably adapted to local administration, for the movies, theaters, safety boxes, clubs, and transactions involving the use of stamps such as mortgage recording, security exchange transactions, and the like, are always in a community capable of establishing adequate administrative controls for the collection of the taxes.

No denial or disclaimer of intent can refute the fact that a federal grant will mean federal control. As the amount of the grant increases, such control will become more certain. And once inaugurated, the amount will surely increase. The salvation of local autonomy in educational matters depends on rejecting, once for all, this Trojan horse of federal support. The right solution is to be found in improving the tax resources of the states and their local units.

PUBLIC HEALTH

The responsibility for health is in part private, in part public. Every person has a duty to himself, to his family, and to the community to take care of his health. That this obligation is often neglected does not diminish either its moral or its economic significance. It is also true that such personal neglect is by no means always associated with lack of income.

The area of public health responsibility includes various broad fields such as sanitation, inspection of foods, water, medicines, and other commodities; the control of contagious diseases by proper segregation; the provision of hospital facilities where this cannot be done by private effort; and specialized research into the causes and possible cures of disease.

The major issue to be dealt with here is the effort that is being made to extend the domain of public health to include governmental administrative and financial responsibility for those aspects of individual and family health which should continue to be assumed by each person for himself.

THE PRESSURE to extend federal participation in the administration and financing of health care is a product of the well-organized movement to erect a totalitarian state. It is a bare-faced device to gain popular support for complete nationalization by the familiar technique of the fraudulent offer of something for nothing.

In the propaganda for nationalization of health care much is made of the alleged bad state of health of a large part of the population. If this charge were well-founded, supporting evidence would be provided by the death rate. In fact, this rate has declined over the past generation and life expectancy rates have risen. Moreover, a remarkable change has occurred during the past fifty years in the principal causes of death. In 1900 the two major causes of death were: (1) the pulmonary diseases such as tuberculosis and pneumonia; and (2) the enteric diseases such as typhoid and dysentery. These scourges have been brought under control and a case of typhoid is now regarded as a disgrace to any community. Today the principal causes of death are: (1) the various forms of circulatory failure usually lumped together as heart disease; and (2) cancer.

This phenomenal transformation in the character of the health problem has been a product of private medical advance and of competent state and local action. Federal participation has consisted mainly of research conducted by army and navy medical specialists. There can be no objection to continued federal activity in medical research and various specialized federal research institutes have already been established. The record makes no case whatever for a great extension of federal participation and control.

Yet the present campaign for a compulsory federal health "insurance" program goes very much beyond the legitimate area of medical research. It would bring the entire population under another form of federal control and paternalism. The defects of this scheme are so obvious and so serious as to leave no doubt that the ulterior objective is another form of rule through regimentation.

First, there is no need for such drastic action. The public or governmental aspects of health and sanitation are already well organized and well conducted at state and local levels. Except the federal inspection that has long been exercised over foods and drugs in interstate commerce, the maintenance of sanitary conditions in milk and water supplies, public eating houses, housing, manufacturing establishments, and other possible sources of infection or contagion is a function that can be adequately performed only by local authorities with general supervision no farther removed than at the state level. Likewise, contagious disease quarantine must be a local responsibility.

Second, no law, federal, state, or local, can police the basic health habits and practices of 155,000,000 persons. Granted that continued emphasis upon the importance of these matters is highly desirable, this can be done without regimentation, and the objectives cannot be attained through regimentation. Information regarding health matters is now being distributed, and effectively, through various private and public agencies. Complete co-operation is not likely to be secured by any measures, certainly not by a national compulsory plan.

Third, national compulsion is not necessary to secure the benefits of the insurance principle. This is demonstrated by the extensive development of voluntary association plans in which many millions of persons are now enrolled. These voluntary plans are capable of conforming to true insurance principles, namely: (1) that the risk insured against be calculable; (2) that the event or contingency insured against be adverse to the insured's interest; and (3) that the cost be fully covered by the premiums collected.

Fourth, a national compulsory plan would not meet any of these tests. It might appear that if certain risks are calculable for a million persons in a Blue Cross plan, they would be calculable for the whole population in a national plan. But the voluntary plan covers only certain contingencies and these ordinarily involve hospitalization as proof of the illness or injury. A national plan would purport to cover everything for everybody.

Universal coverage of everything for everybody would defeat the actuarial calculation of risk, and thus it would defeat the other tests. There would be no possible way to control the chiseling and malingering, for the universal dispensing of pills, medical visits, and even wigs, dentures, and spectacles, as in England, is not adverse to the insured's interest. It quickly becomes a right.

Without effective control the cost of such a program would shortly exceed the premium receipts. National compulsion is not based merely on the proposition to provide certain medical materials and services to the people because government can do this job more efficiently, and hence at lower cost, than is now the case under the existing private auspices. Rather, its essence involves the provision of medical and hospital services at less than cost, at nominal cost, or at no cost, to the recipients. But the cost will fall somewhere, and as the English experiment shows, it will in time fall on the recipients, but only after they have gone too far to draw back.

Fifth, national compulsion is, in reality, just another battalion of the shock troops that socialism is sending into the fight against freedom. Its pretense of aiding the so-called "underprivileged" is fraudulent. Even the lowest income groups must now surrender upwards of one quarter of their income to support government. When the burden of government is reduced, everyone will have more of his income left to meet his own obligations and far more incentive to do so. Whether, even in such improved circumstances, there will be generally increased concern with health matters will depend on the individual and on his response to the sound advice now available. Compulsion will not generate this change of attitude nor would the supposedly free pills of socialized medicine accomplish it.

THE DEPENDENCY PROBLEM

Dependency, like health, is partly an individual, and partly a social, responsibility. That is, granted that there is a public obligation to care for those who, in given circumstances, cannot support themselves, the primary obligation to do this is on the individual with respect to himself and such family dependents as he may have. The obligation of society, whether through private philanthropy or through government, should be residual, not primary.

The fashionable current doctrine is, however, that the primary obligation is on government rather than on the individual. Public welfare policy and program are, in effect, designed to promote rather than discourage reliance on government.

Again, the major issue is the place of the federal government in the performance of such relief services as may, under any view of the case, devolve upon the public authorities. The position taken here is that this is essentially a state and local job. As a matter of administration such is necessarily the case. It can be so from the standpoint of financing also, by releasing to the states sufficient tax resources to perform it.

DEPENDENCY, which means the inability of the individual or the family to supply his or its economic needs, has many forms or aspects. At any time from cradle to grave economic vicissitudes may overwhelm. Misfortune may strike the young, the middle-aged, or the old. Illness, death of the breadwinner, unemployment, enforced retirement at a specific age—any of these or a combination of them, may produce circumstances in which an individual or a family becomes dependent on aid from outside sources.

While it is important to point out the distinction between the individual attitudes of prudence and imprudence that have a significant quantitative bearing on the issue of public aid, this is not the matter of primary concern here. Rather, the real issue involves first, a question of theory and policy regarding public aid, and second, a question of administrative jurisdiction over that part of the dependency relief responsibility which, by general agreement, devolves upon government.

With respect to the question of theory and policy, let it be granted at once that there is a public obligation to rescue the citizens, even the most wayward and improvident, from hunger, illness, and lack of decent shelter and clothing. But the concession of this public obligation raises at once another point—does the admitted *obligation* automatically and necessarily imply the creation of a parallel right of the beneficiaries to receive? The following statement from a publication of the Social Security Board is indicative of the official attitude:

If, as public assistance administrators, we have genuine conviction as to the applicant's rightful claim on society in time of need, if our feelings about this principle are not divided, we will be inclined to think and feel in terms of the applicant's needs and be less protective of the taxpayer.

And **again**, from the same publication:

Social security and public assistance programs are a basic essential for attainment of the socialized state envisaged in democratic ideology, a way of life which so far has been realized only in slight measure. *

It would be difficult to express more forcefully than the above excerpts do the current emphasis upon the *right* to receive, and the reasons therefor, as against the community *obligation* to provide.

Now, without any exploration of the myriad reasons that may underlie the inability of a certain proportion of the population to provide adequately for their own support at any given time, the fact remains that during their dependency

---

* *Common Human Needs*. An Interpretation for Staff in Public Assistance Agencies. Federal Security Agency, Social Security Board, Bureau of Public Assistance Report No. 8, pp. 23, 57.

status they are nonproducers. The doctrine of a *right* to receive means that nonproducers have, automatically, legally, and morally, a *right* to share in the product of the producers. And in proportion as the concern of the public assistance administrators for the producer-taxpayers declines (as the Social Security Board document quoted above counsels) the more imperative—and impertinent—will become the insistence on the "right to share." Such a doctrine would be valid only in a communist state that adhered rigidly to the theoretically perfect communist philosophy—"from each according to ability, to each according to need." Realistic communism, so far as we have seen it in action, rejects such idealistic, perfectionist nonsense. In Russia, those who do not work do not eat very much. Yet, this doctrinaire communist equalitarianism is a guiding tenet of our own Federal Security Agency.

With respect to the jurisdiction—federal, state, or local—to which should be allocated the administrative responsibility for the various aspects of aid that are to be handled by public authority, there is only one test. It is this—if there is any part of the public relief job that is reasonably foolproof and that also involves problems and issues of nation-wide concern, such part can be relegated to federal administration. Any part of the job that cannot decisively and conclusively meet this test should be relegated to state and local jurisdiction.

OLD AGE AND SURVIVORS' BENEFITS

The broad field of federal participation in dependency support has been divided, by federal legislation, into the following areas: (1) old age and survivors' benefits; (2) certain aid categories for which federal grants are made to the states, namely, dependent children, the blind, and the needy not covered by any of the preceding provisions; (3) the unemployed.

The financing methods differ for each of these areas.

Old age and survivors' benefits are a charge on employers and employees in "covered" industries at an equal percentage payable by each on wages or salaries up to an annual maximum which is now $3,600. Unemployment compensation is a charge on payroll borne entirely by the employers (except in four states where employees also contribute). The federal grants to states for dependent children, the blind, and the needy come from general funds.

Complete federal administration is now restricted to old age and survivors' benefits. This part of the relief job meets the test suggested above. It is the only part of the job that does. It should be the limit of federal administrative participation.

THE OLD AGE and survivors' benefit system is reasonably well adapted to federal administration. This is because the primary basis of eligibility for benefits, namely age, is a fact about the individual that does not invite an excessive or uncontrollable degree of deceit to the advantage of the individual. There is considerable coyness about disclosure of age but this is in the direction of under- rather than over-statement of the correct age. Such deceit, whether from false pride or other reasons, does not lead to heavier payments from the Treasury.

On the other hand, every other aspect of the relief and dependency problem presents opportunities for individual gain at the public expense that are not detectable or controllable under federal administration. This is true of illness, accident, unemployment, and general dependency. Effective, impartial administration of these forms of dependency relief must be essentially local, with general oversight no farther removed than the state level. Adequate funds for these purposes can be provided by state, or combined state and local revenue measures, once the scope and cost of federal responsibilities have been reduced as they should be and can be. It is only because we have been blinded by the illusion that federal money is free money that the wasteful and costly system of federal grants-in-aid has become so entrenched.

The federal old age benefit system is a mixture of contributory pension and relief. Both employers and employees in covered industry contribute to the cost, but the benefit formula continues to be weighted heavily in favor of those with low incomes. The basic fact is that the working part of the population is supporting the nonworking part. This is always true, whether such support is at haphazard or is systematized under a contributory process.

This central fact is obscured by the erroneous characterization of the old age benefit system as insurance. In consequence of this confusion, the law has always imposed rates of tax on employers and employees far higher than would be necessary to provide the benefits currently payable. This procedure has been accepted because the workers subject to the old age taxes appear to hold the belief that they are building up a fund that will actually be paid out to them upon retirement.

The insurance reserve fund concept is wholly inapplicable here. In private insurance a certain group of policyholders pay premiums that are invested, as a reserve, in economic claims against the rest of the economy, such as bonds, mortgages, and corporation stocks. From their standpoint the reserve is a necessary and valid protection. But the whole nation cannot create a reserve of invested premiums in the same sense. There is no outside group against which, by appropriate investment, an economic claim can be established. The claim can only be against themselves, collectively. The only genuine protection that can be assured to as large a proportion of the working population as is now covered by the old age and survivors' benefit program is that which comes from the continued willingness and capacity of the people to pay taxes.

In other words, the cost of the benefits now payable should be put on a current, pay-as-we-go basis. This means that there should be collected, each year, from employers and employees, no more than is required to meet the benefits payable in that year. In view of the shortcomings of budget projections, this general rule would not be violated by setting the rates of pay-roll tax to produce approximately the amounts required and by changing these rates at two or three year intervals. Variations in the amount of payroll tax and in the annual benefit payments might produce moderate excesses of receipts or payments from year to year. A firm objective should be, first, not to let the collections lag so much as to cause a permanent increase of debt, and second, not to let them so exceed payments as to pile up large revenue surpluses from this source.

Maintenance of the old age and survivors' benefit system on a current cash basis would involve a gradual increase in the rates of payroll tax. This would continue through the first generation of the system's operation. The reason would be that with time the number of aged eligible persons would increase until at last a balance would be struck between beneficiaries and workers. The marked increase in life expectancy is likely to result in a relative increase of the aged population for some time to come. The level at which a stabilization of the necessary tax rates would occur is not now predictable.

Two arguments have been advanced against the tax rate reduction that would be involved now in a pay-as-we-go plan. The first is that the resistance would be lessened to inordinate increases in current benefits. It is argued that the tax rates must be raised with every increase of benefits in order to keep the latter within bounds.

This argument overlooks the fact that one group is now paying the taxes and another group is getting the current benefits. The social security taxpayers are not now beneficiaries. There is no convincing logical connection between the taxes and the benefits. There would be such a connection if the taxes now paid were determined directly by the current cost of the benefits. Those who are concerned with this aspect of the matter would do well to consider that the workers who are now paying the social security taxes would be more likely to demand prudent determination of benefits if there were an immediate reflection of any increase in the tax rates than when there is no demonstrable connection, which is the case now.

A second argument is that under a cash basis relation between the taxes and the benefits, it may eventually be necessary to increase the payroll taxes to a level higher than the workers are willing to pay.

Whether or not this will happen will depend mainly on the scale of benefits. It seems certain that the number of beneficiaries will increase, and as this occurs the amount that can be paid to each must have careful attention, lest the total bill should exceed what the workers are prepared to set aside for this purpose. But it must be emphasized that even if there be rebellion against further advances of the payroll taxes, the workers and their employers will still be paying the great bulk of the bill for the dependents, whatever it may be.

A final consideration is suggested by this prospect of steadily rising costs. It is the possibility that eventually there must come a revision of the system whereby the benefits will be payable on a need basis, and not to all covered workers, as at present.

PUBLIC ASSISTANCE

Few would deny the existence of a public obligation to relieve distress by providing assistance to the needy—children, the blind, the aged, and others incapacitated by illness or other causes. This major thesis is not at issue here. Rather, the discussion will involve two matters that are of first importance, even though they are collateral to the main proposition. These important related matters are:

First, should the federal government have any authority

to shape or control the administration of relief services by the state and local governments?

Second, is it necessary that the states and their local units receive federal grants-in-aid to cover part of the financial cost involved?

In short, should not the federal government withdraw from this field completely?

THE ANSWER to the first and second questions is in the negative. In practice, the major administrative responsibility for all forms of public assistance has been with the states and their local units from the beginning of large-scale public participation in the cost of the various aspects of the general relief problem. This was so obviously the proper solution that direct federal administrative action was never seriously considered. The investigation required prior to the granting of assistance, in cash or in kind, can be properly done only at the local level —by case workers of a municipal or other local district welfare organization. If there is to be an element of sympathy and personal understanding, it must be supplied by persons who know the local conditions and surroundings thoroughly. Likewise, the establishment of need as a condition precedent to assistance grants involves on-the-spot inquiry.

Federal grants in support of these relief services were initiated as a device to persuade all of the states to act promptly in setting up the administrative machinery through which to provide assistance to the needy in an orderly and systematic way. We need not now debate the actual necessity of the grant as a means of securing general state action. The important point is that the states do now have departments or agencies responsible for handling or supervising the relief services, and there is some kind of local organization—urban, rural, or district—that does the administrative routine. The original basis for the grant no longer exists.

The case for the federal grant in aid of relief services rests in part on the illusion that federal money is free money, and in part on the alleged inability of the states and localities to do the financing from tax resources available to them.

Neither side of this argument is valid. As we have said more than once in the earlier discussion, all federal money comes from the people either as taxes or loans. The citizens are really carrying the relief burden along with all other government costs. Their tax load is so much the heavier because they must supply the funds that come back to them as grants. Elimination of the federal grants, accompanied by an equivalent reduction of the federal tax load, would at least enable the states to assume the full cost of relief without an over-all increase of the tax load now being carried.

But much more than the tax relief represented by the relief grants is in prospect as the scope and cost of the federal government are reduced to the dimensions they should have. Elimination of these grants and the amount of taxation they represent is a good way to begin with the larger task of reallocation of service responsibilities and fiscal resources upon which a substantial measure of tax reduction depends.

Another factor points clearly to the need of eliminating the federal relief grants. This is the tendency to federal control that is manifest in all grants. From the outset there has been federal prescription of certain terms and conditions to be complied with if the state were to receive the grant. By administrative interpretation the secrecy of the relief rolls was also made a condition. This rule was broken by the intransigence of the State of Indiana and it was abrogated by Act of Congress in 1951.

The tendency to increase the federal share of the minimum grant has produced some unfortunate results. For many years the federal share was half of a specified minimum. This 50-50 formula has been changed to require the federal government to provide more than half of a certain part. In the case of the needy aged, for example, the federal share is three quarters of the first $20, and half of the remainder to a maximum monthly grant of $50. The effect in some sections has been to relax the eligibility tests and to admit large numbers to the relief rolls. This reaction stems, of course, from the illusion that federal money is free money.

UNEMPLOYMENT COMPENSATION

The third welfare area that has been systematically underwritten by the federal government on a large scale is unemployment. As in the case of the other aspects of dependency relief discussed above, there is no quarrel here with the policy of providing aid during limited periods of unemployment. The sole issue to be considered is whether the administrative responsibilities involved shall be carried by the several states or by the federal government. The states have had administrative jurisdiction since the inception of the present unemployment compensation system, despite periodically resumed efforts by the proponents of big government to transfer this job to federal control. They should continue to have this responsibility.

FEDERAL CONTROL of the system of unemployment relief, or "compensation," as it is called, is to be opposed on the general ground that it would be another step in the direction of centralization. Every such move must be opposed, and especially where it can be shown that the rights, interests, and well-being of the people are adequately protected by state action. In the present case the large part played by the states from the beginning demonstrates their right and their competence to continue. The following facts indicate the wisdom of the course that has been followed.

First, the payroll tax paid by employers to supply the funds is a state tax. When the system was inaugurated an overriding federal payroll tax was imposed, with provision for a credit up to 90 per cent of the federal tax for any similar tax levied by the states. The original purpose was to persuade—or to compel—the states to act promptly in accepting the system. The theory of the federal claim to 10 per cent of the tax (i.e., .3 per cent of an overriding federal tax of 3 per cent) has been that this fund would be the source of a federal grant to the states to defray the administrative costs of the unemployment compensation system.

Thus a degree of federal control has been retained, a characteristic of all grants. The federal share of the payroll tax has, however, greatly exceeded the grants for administrative costs. The excess has been used for general federal expenses. From 1935 to 1950 the total collected ostensibly for this purpose but not actually devoted to it has been $1,196 million.

Second, the actual verification of the fact of unemployment is necessarily a task for local investigators, supervision of which should in no case be farther removed than the state level. An important criterion for certification of unemployment payments is the possibility of alternative employment, which involves a co-ordinate system of employment offices through which available job opportunities in the locality can be cleared.

Unless the compensation system and the employment service are closely integrated at the local level, there can be no effective control. It is true that abuses have developed in state administration, but there can be no doubt that far greater abuses would have occurred, and would have been tolerated, if the whole system had been under federal control. The fact that much more has been consistently collected in payroll taxes than has been required for current benefits, even under the merit rating devices used by the states and sanctioned by federal law, has probably been a factor in such state administrative laxity as has emerged.

Third, the several states have always set their own terms of unemployment compensation, including such matters as amount and duration of benefits, waiting period, and other eligibility provisions. This is logical, for there is no case for a completely uniform system in view of the wide sectional differences in wage rates and living costs. Moreover, an interstate clearing system has been developed to protect those whose wage credits were accumulated in one state but who find themselves unemployed in another state.

Like all other aspects of public welfare support, the cost of unemployment relief should be on a current cash basis. That is, the tax collection in each year should be no more than is required to pay the benefits of that year. It has been implicit from the beginning that this system has been intended only to bridge over temporary out-of-work conditions. The benefit period nowhere includes more than 26 weeks, and the average duration of benefit payments in the fiscal year 1951 was 12 weeks. There has never been an idea that this program could support a large number of unemployed through a prolonged depression period.

In view of the stopgap nature of the program, the states can manage their own financing and they should be given the full responsibility for doing so. This involves complete custody of all funds collected, full determination of the terms of benefit payment, and elimination of the overriding federal tax with federal grants toward administrative costs. Such federal control as may have seemed necessary in inaugurating the system is no longer warranted, for it is now most unlikely that any state would move to repeal its own law if this control were removed.

THE FEDERAL GOVERNMENT AS TRUSTEE

That part of the welfare and relief system which was established by federal action in the middle 1930's has given rise to a peculiar illusion regarding the federal government as trustee. It is generally believed that by collecting more from certain groups of workers and their employers for old age or unemployment benefits than is being currently paid out in benefits, there can be a storage or accumulation of the excess receipts as a reserve against future benefit liabilities. The only practical way by which this reserve can be accumulated is to represent it by special forms of federal debt obligation, since a hoard of money or of bank deposit credits in the amount involved would sterilize the economy.

This debt paper is regarded as an asset, which gives rise to the anomaly of the government's own promises to pay, i.e., its debt, being an asset against another obligation that the government has assumed. This would not make sense in the case of an individual or a business concern. Nor does it make sense in the case of the government. The only sound way to handle a widespread benefit system such as that now operative here is to put it on a current cash basis, with no more revenue collected from the people each year than is required by the benefit payments of that year.

THE ILLUSORY character of the federal trust accounts as a "reserve" can be seen from a brief outline of the process whereby they are created. In the case of the old age and survivors' benefit system, for example, a tax is levied at the rate of 3 per cent on the first $3,600 of wages, or on such part thereof, as is paid to an employee in the course of a year. Workers and employers pay 1½ per cent each. The worker's share is withheld and sent to the Treasury in connection with the income tax returns.

As this particular tax is collected it is accounted for by the bookkeeping operation of transfer to the old age and survivors' trust fund. This simply means that the Treasury keeps the actual cash and delivers to the trust fund its special debt paper for the requisite amount, after charging for the benefits being currently paid by the Federal Security Administrator. All of the other benefit programs, such as unemployment compensation, veterans' insurance, and the various civil service pension and retirement funds, are handled in the same way.

The real significance lies in the fact that there is no "money" in any of the trust accounts, nor can there be. The only thing in them is some government debt. This debt is not even marketable; it cannot be sold directly to banks or other investors. To whatever extent it should ever become necessary to draw upon any of the so-called reserves, the Treasury would first have to sell other bonds or notes to the people and use the cash thus obtained to redeem the special debt in the trust funds. It would be possible, of course, to get the needed cash by increasing taxes. But whether taxes or loans are used, it becomes clear that the real reserve is the continued ability and willingness of the people to carry the load.

The nation as such does not have, nor can it have, any other reserve against all of its commitments. Certainly the taxes now being paid for these various benefit and welfare purposes in excess of current benefit outgo do not constitute any part of that future taxable capacity which must be drawn upon when a phantom reserve must be liquidated.

The idea that there is a parallel between the reserve accumulated by a private insurance company and a reserve which the nation builds up in its own debt has added to the confusion. A private company insures only a part of the whole population. Its investments in bonds, mortgages, and other earning assets are claims against the income produced by others. The government bonds it owns are claims against the taxes paid by all the people. But the nation includes all of the people and its reserve is its claim against the income of the people. There is no one outside an insured group that includes all the people who can be called upon to provide income for it. Therefore the debt paper in a trust account is plain foolishness. The nation has plenary taxing power and can collect what it needs. The paper in the trust accounts is wastepaper.

The whole approach should be changed. The economic fact should be recognized that the workers—including employers and employees—must produce the goods and services for their own support and for the support of the nonworkers—the aged, the young, the sick, the disabled, and the unemployed. That is, the relief system must operate within the price and money economy. Insofar as public provision of the requisite money income to the nonworkers is a part of policy, it should be done by a current levy on those who pay taxes. And there is no case for collecting more tax for this specific purpose than may be needed for the current volume of benefits. In other words, just as part of the product must go to the nonworkers for their support, so also must part of the income go to them in order that they may buy what they are to get.

The rate of this tax will have to rise as the case load of beneficiaries increases. The objection offered here to the present system is that the workers are being compelled to pay much more tax now than is really required.

The present system derives its popular support largely from the false impressions established. The workers submit to a rate of payroll tax far in excess of what is needed because they appear to believe that they are laying up treasure for the future. In reality, they are providing large sums for general governmental use if there is a budget deficit; or, at best, for the retirement of other debt if the budget is otherwise in balance. Some may regard this as good policy, but candor requires that those who are thus serving as financial pillars of the government should clearly understand the situation.

FULL EMPLOYMENT

A recent legislative expression of paternalism is "full employment" by fiat or decree. The act establishing this so-called policy was passed at a time when it was believed that the end of the war would be followed by depression and large-scale unemployment. This pessimistic view, which had no foundation of sound economic analysis at the time and was wholly refuted by later developments, was responsible for other legislation designed to support the economy by large spending programs. It was the basis, also, for presidential support of the first rounds of the spiral of wage increases.

The economic significance of the Full Employment Act has never been carefully or completely thought through. It was, in one sense, an emotional product that stemmed from the depressed 1930's, and in another sense it was an outcrop of the rampant centralizing forces of the war period. It is a prime expression of the aims of the planned, controlled economy.

THE IMPORTANCE of jobs for all who are able and willing to work is obvious. The extent and the cost of dependency relief in its major forms are connected with the supply of available work opportunities. The issues involved are: (1) What is "employment"? (2) In any true meaning of the term can government provide it, beyond the normal quantity of personnel required to perform the necessary public services? (3) What kind of action or policy, if any, is it proper for government to apply in the interest of attaining full employment?

As the term "employment" is used here, it means being engaged in some task or occupation of economic significance, i.e., that a product of value is being created in the performance of this task or occupation. The "employed" person receives income—normally wages, salary, or commissions—in return for the manual or mental effort that he devotes to production. Value created, and income received through employment, are thus the two sides of the shield. It should be noted, however, that no given echelon of workers—as in a particular factory or assembly plant—can be credited with producing the entire value of the output of this factory or plant. They work on materials supplied by workers elsewhere, and they use tools, machinery and other plant equipment supplied by those who save and invest. The final value of product must cover material costs, direct and indirect wages in the particular plant, interest on capital, profit, and taxes.

In the private economy the market place provides a clean-cut, objective test of the relationship between income received and value created through employment. If a sufficient value has been created, the goods or services produced will be useful enough to someone to induce him to exchange part of his income for them. The goal of "full employment" is attained when there are work opportunities for all in producing useful things and when these things are regularly disposed of in the market. It is generally agreed that there will be at all times a certain number of persons who are temporarily not employed because of technological changes, transfers from one job to another, regional migration, and illness. These factors together could account for as much as 5 per cent of the labor force without jeopardy to the practical full employment objective.

Employers and workers alike have responsibilities for the attainment and maintenance of reasonably full employment. The employer, as entrepreneur and manager, should channel employment into the lines of production where the prospects of sale are brightest. He has the further obligation to present the product effectively through sound sales promotion. The workers' joint responsibility is primarily that of avoiding wage demands so extreme as to price their product out of the market.

In the light of the foregoing definition of employment, the answer to the question of whether government can provide employment is self-evident. True, a certain number of persons is required to perform the necessary public services, but there is no objective market test of the value of their services because the people are compelled to pay the cost through taxation. Granting, however, that there would be little objection to paying taxes for the cost of the proper and necessary services of government, the issue becomes acute when a vast expansion of public personnel and payroll beyond this level is contemplated, as would be the case if government were to undertake a guarantee of full employment regardless of the cost or the values created.

The government can, of course, add large numbers to the public payroll, and it can spend huge sums on contracts for the construction of all manner of public works. There cannot be an objective, market place test of the value created, and in substantial degree that which is thus provided is not "employment" but a form of relief, hidden under the cloak of wage rates and hours corresponding to those currently prevailing.

Public provision of employment on any large scale is very likely to bypass citizen approval or disapproval, which would normally be expressed in the attitude toward the taxes required to pay the bills. This bypass would be arranged by increasing the public debt to cover a substantial part of the cost. In short, any serious attempt by government to attain the goal of full employment through its own efforts to provide "employment" would almost certainly involve inflationary debt increase. The burden of this method of payment would fall immediately on certain segments of the economy, and eventually on all. In the end the fraudulent character of the policy would become plain to all, but the damage done could not then be corrected.

Since a government guarantee of full employment cannot be made good except by an inflation that will be injurious, eventually, to all, it follows that no such guarantee should be given. The kind of policy that would be most conducive to attainment of bona fide full employment must be characterized by restraint, not by direct action. The burden of government itself must be reduced. The people must be allowed to keep and spend more of the income they earn. There must be an end to governmental interference, regulation, and persecution of private business for partisan political advantage, or for furtherance of the objectives of the planned economy. Above all, there must be an end to the inflation that is always fomented by the inability or unwillingness of the Congress to keep the budget in balance. The doctrine of government-supported full employment is a social psychosis produced by the decade of depression and mass unemployment during the 1930's. The seeds of any depression are to be found in the preceding boom and inflation. If we are to avert the excesses of depression we must avoid the excesses of the prior boom and inflation. Government can do more now to prevent future large-scale unemployment by bringing its finances under control and by allowing the banking system to exercise a prudent restraint on private credit, than by any other measures available to it.

PLANT SEIZURE

This nation is at deadly grips with destructive forces. The core and essence of freedom is the *right* to own. Government seizure of private property under vague and indefinite powers allegedly bestowed by the Constitution is a direct and flagrant violation of that right, and it is, therefore, a direct attack upon the citadel of individual freedom.

THE RIGHT of government to take and use private property, under certain circumstances, and on terms prescribed by the Constitution, is old and well established. Martial law, which means the right and power of a military government to supersede the power and authority of the civilian governments, is a thoroughly established principle. Under martial law the military—whether it be the state national guard or some unit of federal military authority—has the power to requisition supplies, to occupy and manage private property such as buildings and equipment, to impress citizens into various kinds of labor service, and in every respect to act and operate as a military dictatorship.

With this general concept we have no quarrel. When an emergency exists, and when the lives and fortunes of all of us depend on the outcome, there must be a central authority to apportion tasks and resources. Perhaps we have been wrong all this time in calling it "martial law." Maybe what has been striven for, namely, a competent authority, could have been provided under civilian auspices. But in view of the fact that the principal solvent in any situation that requires resort to such action is force, and in view of the further fact that the principal source of such force that any government has at its disposal is its armed forces, it is no doubt logical enough that whatever order, security, and policing that appear necessary be provided by calling out regiments of troops and giving the commanders of these troops authority to make, for the time being, the laws and ordinances under which the people shall live.

What we are dealing with here is a far cry from martial law, although the federal legislation under which the government has been authorized to "seize" private property obviously stemmed, at the outset, from the accepted concept of martial law. That is, the whole emphasis during World War II and in the Selective Service Act of 1948 was upon the authority that the government should have in the event that any private citizen—individual, partnership, or corporation—should refuse or fail to supply the government with goods or services that he or it could produce and that the government deemed essential to its war or defense effort. This was the authority to seiz the plant and productive facilities of such firm and operate them in order that the essential needs of the government might be met.

This is in accord with the general principle of martial law stated above. But the procedure has been deviously and subtly perverted. The perversion consists in using the seizure power as a means of determining the outcome of disputes between labor and management over wages, hours, and other terms of the employment contract, or current renewals thereof.

We can dispose quickly of the superficial aspects of such conflicts. One is the alleged insecurity of workers who continue to work without a contract. This has always been a fraudulent contention, for there has never been a possibility that workers would not be paid, whether a contract applied to the work period or not. There is plenty of state law relating to mechanics' liens to protect them, with or without a specific contract.

The second superficial aspect of these conflicts is whether the government would really be deprived of goods and services vital to its national purposes. The obvious answer is that there would be no deprivation as long as production continued.

A third superficial aspect is the fanciful notion that workers will not strike against the government. In the light of experience this is pure fairy tale that should deceive no one.

We are not concerned here with the merits of the issue in any particular case of government seizure. The situation is far more serious than this. What we should be deeply concerned about is the series of dress rehearsals of the national socialist state that this foolish, indefensible policy of government seizure provides. If the government can seize all of the private property in one industry, under as flimsy pretexts as are now being employed, it can seize all private property in all industries. And in view of the grounds that have served in recent cases of seizure, similar pretexts could easily be produced throughout industry. If these flimsy pretexts are allowed to prevail as the excuse to seize, what is to prevent their invocation? And what is the assurance that government seizure will ever be ended? The government has been the technical owner of the railroads for some two years now, with no date set for termination of this technical ownership.

The fact is that there are various procedures short of seizure for the orderly settlement of the wage disputes that have become a fixed feature of the perennial demonstration of the power of the labor bosses over their followers and the economy. If these procedures are deficient they should be corrected. It is not only foolish, but dangerous, to go through the motions of the totalitarian state as a gesture. Sooner than we think someone then in authority may take the gesture as a serious matter. There should be prompt enactment of legislation to deny to any federal administration the authority to seize private property for any purpose short of the kind of situation under which martial law might properly be invoked. And if there should develop a national emergency so serious as to warrant resort to martial law for the nation, the case for it would have to be so evident and obvious that no general dissent could develop.

Obviously, however, no such case could be made if martial law were to be invoked to execute the findings of any government board in any particular industrial wage dispute.

The real issue is much more important. Government seizure is a denial of the right of individuals to own, and to this extent, it is an invasion of their freedom. There would be a fight to a finish if government were to impound wages; how is it different when government impounds the plant that is owned by thousands of separate, though unorganized persons, the stockholders of the company, and which is, moreover, the principal means by which the wages are earned? The worker who regards with glee or unconcern government seizure of his company's plant should keep in mind that a dictatorship does not distinguish between one form and another of the right to own. When government owns the plant he may be compelled to work there for whatever wage his master may decree, or for his keep. Remember always that there are no racial or national differences in men drunk with power. We still have the capacity, and God willing, the will to resist. In the whole history of slavery, there is no record of a worse master than the state.

CONCLUSION

THE AIM, in this series of short essays, has been to bring into focus the most important issue in the world today. It is the issue of freedom versus slavery.

Many are concerned about this matter and about its outcome. But while they are intuitively aware of impending danger, they have neither an adequate perception of its nature nor a sufficient intellectual and moral defense against it.

So, to provide an armament against the assault on freedom, it was necessary to begin with a restatement of the essence of freedom. It is the *right* to own. On this rock all other aspects, attributes, and elements of freedom are built.

Government does not create this right. Rather, its principal function is to protect it, by establishing justice under law, by maintaining internal order and security, and by effective defense against external aggression. Only a stable government can give this protection and the ultimate test of governmental stability is the capacity to manage properly the public finances.

On the other hand, government can undermine the *right* to own, by overt acts of destructive taxation, intolerable regulation, and erosion of values through inordinate public borrowing; and also by covert seductions of public generosity whereby the significance of this right is diminished. All forms of collectivism involve diminution, and eventual denial, of the right of individual ownership. They therefore lead, by one path or another, to the loss of personal freedom by abrogation of its foundation.

111

But the terms "the government" and "the state" are abstractions. The concrete, operating entity is the political party in power. The dictators have always decreed that the party is the state, by which they have meant a permanent fusion of the party and the abstract concept of the state. Here, it is true that the party in power is, in effect, the government for its acts and decisions (laws, regulations, and administrative policies) are the only visible and tangible evidence that any citizen can ever have of the existence, presence, and purposes of the state. The great difference is that we have not accepted a complete fusion of one particular party with the state, but are still free to change the party in power.

Our political parties are efficiently organized and managed so far as concerns the periodic struggle for offices and for the temporal power gained by success in these contests. They are almost wholly deficient in the sense of responsibility and in the effective party discipline that are required in view of the fact that the party in power is the government in action.

The path of least resistance for the party in power is to seek perpetuation of its control by exchanging benefits for votes. This is also the path of complete disregard of party responsibility if we assume that government exists to protect freedom and not to destroy it. The inevitable price of the benefits is a further expansion of the size, power, and cost of government with a consequent expansion of the domination of government over the freedom of the individual.

The preservation of our freedom must be achieved in and through a political party, because the party in power is all that anyone ever sees, or comes in contact with, in his effort to reach that intangible and abstract something called "the government." If freedom is lost, scuttled, or whittled away, it will be a result of the policies, intentional or inadvertent, of the party in power. Our future, our freedom, and our fortunes are always in the hands of the party in power. Those who have been too busy making money, or following the sports events, or just having fun, to attend to what the party in power, acting as their government, is about, would better become aware of these facts of life. The "point of no return" has not yet been reached, but every extension of federal power and burden brings us closer to it.

This book offers bitter, but salutary, medicine. Its purpose is to warn the people to beware of a party that emphasizes chiefly what it will do *for* them, and it advises adherence to a party that emphasizes chiefly what it will *not* do *to* them. Both of the major parties have been too free in promising benefits. Neither of them has been willing to risk the temporary loss of leadership by developing a constructive program for the lightening of burdens. Yet it is obvious that the capacity to lead is well demonstrated by the statesmanship displayed in opposition. And what statesmanship could be more appealing and convincing in this time of crushing taxes and flagrantly wasteful government than a program of doing less *for* the people by doing less *to* them? It is plain political and economic arithmetic that no party can do things *for* the people without doing things *to* them.

In all seriousness here, in essence, is the ultimate difference between slavery and freedom. If a party can remain in power indefinitely by always doing more things *for* the people, it will eventually have done enough *to* them in the process of providing the benefits so that, in the end, the final injury—loss of the *right* to own—will have been inflicted.

The logic of this conclusion is clear. As the welfare commitments of government grow, the problem of providing them expands. The right of private ownership and the privilege of individual decision as to the use of what is owned, obviously conflict with that total control of resources which government must eventually exercise in order to fulfill its growing benefit obligations. This pressure will lead, in time, to socialization.

And when the individual's right to own has been taken away, he will have no other rights that anyone need respect. The ethics and morality of our American civilization have been based on the proposition that man, the individual, is a being of dignity, entitled to respect and regard. But with what shabby remnants of worth, dignity, and respect can man be clothed when he no longer has the *right* to own anything?

(1)